CDS, RECORDS, & TAPES

PERSONAL LINER NOTES ON HIP HOP

SABIN PRENTIS

Copyright © 2020 by Sabin Prentis Duncan

Published by Fielding Books, Richmond, VA

ISBN - 13: 978-0-9984885-6-1

All rights reserved

No part of this book may be reproduced in any form by any electronic or mechanical means, including information storage and retrieval systems, without written permission from the author, except for the use of brief quotations in a book review.

Earlier versions of these essays have appeared online.

First edition, 2020

*Dedicated to my brother-in-writing, Ran Walker,
my college roommate & partner-in-music-appreciation, Rashad,
my homeboys, Jason, John, & Mike,
and all the Hip Hop Heads and lovers of good music.*

"When you feel like you can't make work,
make work from work that's already made."

— Questlove; **Creative Quest** (2018)

FOREWORD
RASHAD MOBLEY

There is a never-ending list of fears attached to the first week of attending college - particularly a Historically Black College or University (HBCU). You worry about whether your high school smarts will translate to college success, you worry how quickly you'll make friends, you have grave concerns about clothes being accepted or ridiculed, and there's just an overall malaise about adjusting and thriving in an unfamiliar environment.

But the assimilation of one's music is rarely taken into consideration during this transition and it should be, because it is just as important.

Music is a vital ingredient in this magical elixir we call everyday life. I listen to music while I workout and while I write, others listen to music while they clean or work, and music is universally played in cars, trucks and jeeps. In fact, one of the more joyous times of college life involved coming back home to see my friends and a) sharing the new music that I discovered in college and b) figuring out what local music I had missed. Once that musical determination was made, our car playlist was fully formed, and summer had officially begun.

So back in 1992 when I first started Hampton University and I met my roommate, a young, energetic brother named Sabin Prentis, it took two days for me to realize I was in for a challenging musical journey.

While Sabin had a deep appreciation for old-school R&B the way I did (Barry White, Stevie Wonder, Rolls Royce), he also liked a collection of hip hop artists that were completely foreign to me. Groups like Poison Clan, Home Team, 8Ball and MJG, Detroit's Most Wanted, and Esham. While I was no stranger to profanity and misogyny in music, these groups doubled down on it and then some - often times masking their ability to expertly flow over the beat.

Meanwhile, my hip-hop groups of choice were De La Soul, A Tribe Called Quest, Gang Starr (who Sabin liked at one point, but he abandoned them when the video version of "Just To Get A Rep" greatly differed from the album version) and Redman just to name a few. Those artists weren't exactly spewing Christian rhymes but the language didn't seem as stark and harsh as the music blaring from Sabin's speakers.

Of course, our musical tastes did overlap occasionally. We appreciated the complex lyrical stylings of Rakim and Big Daddy Kane, the storytelling of Ice Cube and Scarface, and the no-nonsense attitudes of EPMD and the Geto Boys.

The differences in our musical tastes, and our willingness to be open to each other's choices (in addition to the tight quarters of our freshman dorm room), allowed for an abundance of teachable moments. Some days my music ruled the day and Sabin voiced his opinion, and I'd defend my selection. Other days he regaled me with his music and

I'd do my best to hate it before succumbing to the beat, the rhymes and the accompanying lessons Sabin gave me.

Fast forward to the year 2020, and our musical tastes mirror each other. We both have occasional bouts of nostalgia and we long for the days when we could listen to Poison Clan with a clear conscience sans the guilt that comes with being fathers, husbands and professional men in our mid 40s. But we also have a great appreciation for the humor and wit of Little Brother, the musicality of The Roots, the soulful sounds of Outkast, and old soul quality of Big K.R.I.T. Music brought us together when we were 18, and now in our 40s, it continues to help define what we're about and more importantly what we write.

So when Sabin critiques, compares and contrasts some of hip hop's biggest offerings from the last 40 years, know that he has been and will continue to be on quite the musical journey. To quote Public Enemy's Flavor Flav, "He don't swear he's nice, he KNOWS he's nice, you know what I'm saying?"

1

RUN DMC THREE-PEAT

RUN DMC ~ KING OF ROCK ~ RAISING HELL

I have been a Hip Hop fan for as long as I have been a basketball fan. I was five years old when I first heard "Rapper's Delight." Earlier that same year, I cheered as the Magic Johnson-led Michigan State Spartans triumphed over the Larry Bird-led Indiana State Sycamores in the NCAA Championship. That next season when they arrived in the NBA, my love for professional basketball was born.

As a NBA fan, I know that winning a championship is a formidable task. Back-to-Back championships are rare. Winning three consecutive championships is exceptionally challenging. Which makes the teams that have accomplished the feat, nearly immortal.

The same could be said for classic Hip Hop albums. Think about it, Das EFX won one championship. Even though I was not a fan of their rhyme scheme, rappers were spitting wiggity-wiggity rhymes for the next year or so after Das EFX's debut. Then there are the back-to-back classics, which I think defines DMX's first two releases. But back-to-back-to-back, the trifecta, a Three-peat? That doesn't happen often.

With this series, we're going to revisit some Hip Hop Three-Peats; yet, here are two things to consider before we proceed:

1. Kendrick Lamar is a Three-peat Champion (**good kid, M.A.A.D. city - To Pimp a Butterfly - Damn.**). Yet, by the time Kendrick was really putting his thing down, I had aged-out of life of the serious purchaser of Hip Hop albums. By acknowledging that limitation of mine, there is no shade to Kendrick because he is remarkable.
2. Golden State Warriors-type perennial top-tier performers who never put together a three-peat. I think this describes Jay-Z, the Roots, and even De La Soul. Steph & Klay (and Durant) did not win three in a row but dude, those cats are legendary.

Now that's that is out of the way, let's roll.

FIRST CHAMPIONSHIP - 1984 - **RUN DMC**

Where We Were:

I think it's safe to say that Run DMC's debut album was the official start of the new school. Much respect to Kool Herc, Grandmaster Caz, Melle Mel, Grandmaster Flash, Cold Crush, and all the forbearers - Run DMC raised an art form from the Bronx and birthed a culture. Back in '82 and '83, cats were looking like Rick James clones. Maybe the outlier was Kurtis Blow, who was cool, but you have to admit when you heard:

I like the pick-and-roll, I like the give-and-go
'Cause it's basketball, uh, Mister Kurtis Blow!

You weren't too sure how long Hip Hop could last.

What made them outstanding:

- Their rhyme pattern - the interplay between them I don't think had been done before.
- The style - these cats looked cool with gear you wanted to wear.
- Their remake of "Hard Times" makes Kurtis Blow's original obsolete.
- The beats - simple drum patterns and rock guitar sound that they pioneered.

What we could have done without:

Album fillers - "Wake Up" and "30 Days."

Championship Moment:

The video for "Rock Box" was on MTV which was unprecedented. Michael Jackson was on MTV and I think maybe Prince was getting some love. But Hip Hop on MTV? Run DMC definitely broke new ground. Regarding the video though, I can't image Jam Master Jay showing love for some random kid at the club. But, I digress, it was the 80s.

How it impacted me:

My brother, Damon, had the cassette and we listened to it on the way to visit his friends. When we arrived, I stayed in the car and replayed the tape over and over until I had it memorized. I could not wait to get to school and be the first one who knew the whole album. I was geeked to proclaim:

> *I'm D.M.C., in the place to be*
> *I go to St. John's University*
> *And since kindergarten I acquired the knowledge*
> *And after 12th grade I went straight to college.*

At nine years old, those bars replaced "I'm here, I'm there, I'm Big Bank Hank I'm everywhere" as my favorites.

SECOND CHAMPIONSHIP - 1985 - **KING OF ROCK**

Where We Were:

It's peculiar that while Run DMC were new school, it seems like they are considered a bridge between the Classic generation and the forthcoming Golden Age. Their delivery had roots in the old-school; yet, they were Hip Hop's first megastars. They changed the game in multiple ways, most notably by attracting the attention of the mainstream.

What made them outstanding:

- No sophomore slump. They improved.
- The swagger / bravado / machismo encapsulated by the B-Boy stance.
- Starring in **Krush Groove** which one-uppped **Beat Street** because it showcased more Hip Hop stars (plus Sheila E. - which is always a good thing).

What we could have done without:

Album filler - "Roots, Rap, Reggae" - If I listened to this album 100 times, I skipped this track 98 of those times.

Championship Moment:

The "King of Rock" video had a couple of moments. It opened with the old cat telling them they did not belong in the Rock museum to which DMC announced:

> *I'm the king of rock, there is none higher*
> *Sucker MCs should call me sire*
> *To burn my kingdom, you must use fire*
> *I won't stop rockin' till I retire!*

Hell yeah! Later, at the video's conclusion, they strutted out the museum with that hip bounce in their stride. I was probably one of many mimicking that strut at school.

How it impacted me:

By this time, Damon and I had perfected our Run DMC reenactments. But when it came to my favorite track, "Darryl and Joe", Damon opted to sit it out. Which made me Run and I declared as passionately as a fifth grader could:

> *I'm the rapper of the year and this the year of*
> *   the rap*
> *And I'm never drinkin' beer, it's champagne at*
> *   the tap*
> *And I'm cold makin' money on a regular basis*
> *Pullin' out knots in sucker MC faces!*

I could not image that they could get much better than that, then they did.

THIRD CHAMPIONSHIP - 1986 - **RAISING HELL**

Where We Were:

Run DMC were established stars and took another quantum leap in popularity by delivering their best album. At the time, it was the biggest Hip Hop album ever and proved to the mainstream that Hip Hop was profitable.

What made them outstanding:

- "My Addias" was both a massive hit and a stroke of marketing genius.
- "Walk This Way" is well-known by non-Hip Hop fans and is the song that catapulted them into mega-stardom.
- One of the most cohesive Hip Hop albums ever.

What we could have done without:

Not applicable - even the fillers were cool.

Championship Moment:

The whole year. Run DMC was everywhere and for us, it was a big "we-told-you-so" to the old heads that said Hip Hop was a passing fad. From videos, tours, endorsements, to TV appearances, Run DMC owned 1986. At the center of all that - was a great album. One that is recognized widely as one of the best ever in any genre.

CDs, Records, & Tapes

How it impacted me:

At eleven years old, I was supposed to be in bed at a certain time. Yet, I did something I had only done with Richard Pryor's **Insane** album, I waited until the hour or two after my mother was asleep but before my dad came home from work. I played the record with my ear glued to the speaker. I must have replayed "Peter Piper" ten times because it made me say

Go*da** that DJ make my day!

Championship Reflection:

Run DMC held it down with three outstanding albums released in three consecutive years. Over time, I heard there were issues impeding the release of their next album **Tougher Than Leather**. Although the single, "Run's House", is a classic; in hindsight, it seems as if music and the Hip Hop sound had passed them by. Many believe that 1988 is one of the best years in Hip Hop. With new styles from Big Daddy Kane and Eric B. & Rakim, Run DMC's rhymes had become dated. A close listen to **Tougher than Leather** supports the idea that had it been released in '87, they could have extended their championship run one more year.

However, from 1984 - 1986, from their self-titled debut- **Run DMC**, to the **King of Rock**, and then **Raising Hell**, Run DMC are Hip Hop's first Three-peat Champions!

So when asked who's the best, y'all should say:
Run-D.M.C. and Jam Master Jay!

2

JUST ONE: JUNE 1988

LONG LIVE THE KANE OR STRICTLY BUSINESS

In June 1988, the summer before I started high school, I faced a choice. A choice that makes up the premise of these Just One essays: only having enough money for one purchase but torn between two recent releases. The June '88 dilemma was choosing between Big Daddy Kane's **Long Live the Kane** and EPMD's **Strictly Business**. That choice is as difficult today as it was then.

To help discern nostalgia from reality, I am going to employ a scoring system. These scoring system will assign 0 - 2 points in four distinct categories. The categories are:

1. *Pre-release history*: What did we know about these groups prior to the reviewed albums' release?
2. *Review of three songs* that either charted highest, had the biggest buzz, or were my favorites.
3. *How did it age / does it still sound fresh?* A good percentage of the Hip Hop Nation has become parents and we often try to extend the excitement we felt about our music to our kids. Sometimes it works and quite often it doesn't. I believe that

one part of it working is musicality. If I hit my kids with Whodini's "One Love", they are rolling with me. If I hit them with Man Parrish's "Boogie Down Bronx" – eh ... let's just say dad gets side-eyes (especially if I try to pop-lock along with it). When compared to Man Parrish, Whodini's music aged better.

4. *Game-Changer or Pace-Keeper*: I believe it is a distinction among classics. For example, Dr. Dre's **The Chronic** is a game-changer. Snoop's **Doggystyle** is a pace-keeper.

In the end, the album with the highest score is the one you and me probably should have purchased first.

Pre-release History

I first saw Big Daddy Kane in the "Biz Is Going Off" video. Soon afterward, Biz's verse and Kane's appearance in the "Vapors" video were my cues that this would be my guy. Again, this is before high school - that time when teens are determining how they want to be seen or accepted. When I saw Kane, I wanted to be that cool. Plus, Biz's line about him fighting everyday had a great bit of personal relevance.

Big Daddy Kane - 2 points

The first time I saw the video for "You Gots To Chill" was the first time I experienced EPMD. I'm not sure if a group could deliver a better introduction than that.

EPMD - 2 points

Song Reviews

"Ain't No Half Steppin" was swagger before we used the term. But more importantly, we were introduced to a top-shelf lyricist. I had already heard Rakim and would not be that awed by an MC until I heard Kane. I really couldn't have counted the number of times I tried to say:

> *The best, oh, yes, I guess, suggest the rest*
>   *should fess*
> *Don't mess or test your highness*
> *Unless you just address with best finesse*
> *And bless the paragraphs I manifest!*

as smoothly as Kane did. He made it seem effortless and cool - yep! this was definitely going to be my role model.

Big Daddy Kane - 2 points, 4 total

"You Gots To Chill" is SLAMMIN'! Numerous artist have used the same Zapp sample but no one has ever hit as hard as these cats did with it. What is remarkable is that their lyrics are not necessarily awe-inspiring but their flow took rather mundane lines like: "if you're tired, then go take a nap" to a whole 'nuther level!

EPMD - 2 points, 4 total

"Raw (remix)": Oh shit. If "Raw" had never been made and a MC spit these rhymes today - they would be an instant YouTube sensation. I mean seriously, it's not a lot of MCs who can top:

Ruling and schooling MC's that I'm dueling
Watch them all take a fall as I sit back cooling
On my throne, with a bronze microphone
Hmm God bless the child that can hold his own...

Big Daddy Kane - 2 points, 6 total

"It's My Thing": Years later, I learned this was their first single. Back in '88, it was my favorite track on the album. What I now know as flow, back then I just thought these dudes were rhyming effortlessly. One indicator of an outstanding artist is that you recognize them as soon as you hear them - EPMD are instantly recognizable.

EPMD - 2 points, 6 total

"Set It Off" follows "Raw" on the album and there is no let down in Big Daddy's lyrical excellence. In "Ain't No Half Steppin'", he mentions opening a school of MCing; which wouldn't be necessary if students studied "Set It Off."

Big Daddy Kane - 2 points, 8 total

"Strictly Business" doesn't have the firepower of "Set It Off" but it is still a gem. It sets the tone for the album. Moreover, I'm willing to bet that I wasn't the only one who wanted a fisherman hat after watching the video.

EPMD - 2 points, 8 total

How Did It Age?

This is really tough. Both sound like late 80's production. While Kane's lyricism is more noteworthy; I don't think its far-fetched to say EPMD are underrated rhymers. All of which to say, sonically - they have aged about the same.

To break this stalemate, we will have to employ the Skip-A-Track Test to distinguish. Both albums have ten tracks and included what was then the obligatory DJ cutting & scratching track. Yet, right now in 2020, you have the remote to an awesome sound system and these albums. For me, I listen to at least 5 from Big Daddy and 4 from EPMD.

> Big Daddy Kane - 2 points, 10 total
> EPMD - 1 point, 9 total

Game-Changer or Pace-Keeper

Considering that there are number of heads that feel that 1988 is the start of the Golden Age of Hip Hop, both of these albums have a hand in that declaration. They did not sound like Run-DMC, Grandmaster Flash & the Furious Five, or even LL Cool J. The beats sounded fresh when compared to early and mid 80s Hip Hop, The wordplay and flow were also a collective improvement from what had been previously released (except **Paid in Full** which is a category all by itself and possibly **Criminal Minded**). I consider them part of the overall game-changing momentum of the times.

> Big Daddy Kane - 2 points, 12 total
> EPMD - 2 points, 11 total

As a 13 year old, I bought Big Daddy Kane. I would make the same choice today. Back then, particularly considering that Big Daddy was the entertainer I admired the most, the idea conveyed by the album cover of some beautiful women feeding me fruit captured my imagination more than sitting in the studio with my mans. I bought EPMD soon thereafter and pronounced that "I'm like Zoro, I'll mark a Z on your back!" Songs from both albums are staples in my current music rotation.

3

BATTLE OF THE POSSE CUTS: CLASSIC EDITION

"THE SYMPHONY" VS. "SCENARIO"

Few things spark a more heated debate between old school Hip-Hop heads than comparing classic Hip-Hop tracks. The Battle of the Posse Cuts is a subjective contest between old school posse cuts. Each contest will adhere to three rules, competing songs:

- Must feature at least three different MCs;
- Cannot be from the same crew (for example Tribe's "Scenario" vs. De La's "Buddy");
- Will be of a similar region (for example TRU's "No Limit Soliders" won't be vetted against Dr. Dre's "Stranded on Death Row").

Each contest will be scored like a relay, the first MC on one track versus the first MC on the second track. As is the case with these songs, some discretion will be applied should the tracks feature a different number of MCs.

Scoring will be simple:

- 0 - Maybe y'all should have just sang the hook;

- 1 - Okay, we hear you;
- 2 - Whoa, that was nice!;
- 3 - DAANNGG, I gotta learn those bars!

Masta Ace vs. Phife Dawg

There is a group of literary types who rave over the opening lines of a book. If the people in that group were Hip-Hop Heads they would get wound-up over Phife's opening:

> *Ayo, Bo knows this (What?)*
> *And Bo knows that (What?)*
> *But Bo don't know jack, 'cause Bo can't rap.*

In 1992, Nike made sure we all knew what Bo knows and at no point did we think Bo could spit. But in case we ever thought so, Phife assures us that Bo can't rap.

Masta Ace opened more subtly when he said:

> *Listen closely, so your attention's undivided*
> *Many in the past have tried to do what I did ...*

It's like he is setting up for a witty punch line that does not deliver a knockout. From the opening bell, Phife's bars are jabbing Masta all over the place. It's almost not even fair. Plus, "Scenario" has a festive, get-amped vibe where the piano lick on "The Symphony"' complements the rhymes. In this head-to-head, Scenario's energy and Phife's flurry of jabs gives the first leg of the relay to Scenario.

Masta Ace - 1 / Phife Dawg - 2
"The Symphony" - 1 / "Scenario" - 2

Craig G vs. Charlie Brown

Charlie Brown gets a nod just for immortalizing North Carolina as 'North Cak-a-laka." I'm from Detroit and until Charlie said it, I ain't never heard nobody nowhere talking about no North Cak-a-laka; but yet, there I was singing along and following North Cak-a-laka with an enthusiastic "COMPTON!"

I suppose that earned him a pass for some of his other bars in the same verse. For example, picture this: me and you in a cipher, right? You're beat-boxing. Our peoples are swaying back and forth and I bust out with "wow-how-now-wow, how now, brown cow!" I think the beat and swaying would stop and the cipher would end. Yet, somehow Charlie made it work. He almost lost us but somehow by adding bass to his voice and shouting "DOO-DOO," he earned a pass.

Craig G came out with some sensible lines. I actually had no idea who he was prior to hearing this track, but just like he predicted, I jumped on the tip when I heard him with the Juice Crew.

In a vacuum, those verses along with Dinco D's wouldn't do much for the listener; but, within these classic tracks, they work. They are the weak legs of the relay, but they work.

> Craig G - 1 / Charlie Brown & Dinco D - 1
> "The Symphony" - 2 / "Scenario" - 3

Kool G Rap vs. Q-Tip

No doubt, Kool G Rap's lisp accentuates his wordplay and Tip's verse feels like an alley-oop to Busta's last verse. The switch-up where Tip and Busta alternate bars increases the anticipation of Busta's finale. "The Symphony" was my introduction to Kool G and I was so impressed I bought the **Road to The Riches** album.

Pound for pound, G Rap's wordplay is tougher and more intricate. Tip's verse rescues us from Dinco's confusing "funk flipped, flat back, first this, foul, fight, fight, fight laugh, yo, how'd that sound?" and sets up Busta for the Ray Allen dagger three-point game-winner from the corner. Without Tip's verse, Scenario would have lost a whole lot of steam. These verses earn a draw.

Kool G Rap - 2 / Q Tip - 2
"The Symphony" - 4 / "Scenario" - 5

Big Daddy Kane vs. Busta Rhymes

Some would argue that this was Kane in his prime, like 2013 LeBron or 2001 Iverson, and I would not disagree. The tired argument that Kane eventually went too hard for the ladies; well, yeah - I mean like Chris Rock, "I ain't saying I agree, but I understand." Anyway, when he said:

> *Battlin' me is hazardous to your health*
> *So put a quarter in your ass, cause ya played*
> *yourself.*

I lost my damn mind. Punchlines like that make him a Hall-of-Fame Top 5 MC. That verse is what makes "The Symphony" a classic. It would take a force of nature to bypass that.

A force of nature is exactly what Busta's verse on "Scenario" proved to be. It was "BOOM from the canon!" That verse on a song where everyone was already jumping around, made all of us jump higher and be more animated. I mean "Oh My Gosh OH MY Gosh!"

In no way am I saying Busta is a better lyricist than Big Daddy. It is indisputable that Big Daddy Kane is a premier MC. However, Busta's delivery on this verse is iconic. It is a Hip-Hop milestone. It catapulted him into a higher realm of celebrity and sparked numerous guest appearances. Kane is cooler than a fan and he delivered his lyrically potent verse as such. But Busta literally changed the game with that animated verse. His career and Hip-Hop would never be the same.

That verse helps "Scenario" nudge by "The Symphony." It takes an one of the all-time most memorable verses in Hip-Hop history to dethrone the Juice Crew.

Big Daddy Kane - 3 / Busta Rhymes - 3
"The Symphony" - 7 / "Scenario" - 8

4
JUST ONE: SEPTEMBER 1988
EASY-DUZ-IT OR POWER

September 13, 1988, a handful of days before my 14th birthday and while I had a few ends in my pocket, I only had enough money to make one purchase. The dilemma I faced over thirty years ago is the focal point of this essay - whose album should I purchase Eazy E or Ice T?

Let's acknowledge that many were moved by Ice T's **Power** album cover. The layout is simple. It's iconic. And most importantly, Darlene was (is) sho'nuff beautiful. For right now though, we are going to try to pretend that was not a factor in the choice.

Like before, we will employ some reflective variables that should help us choose whether **Eazy-Duz-It** or **Power** should have been our initial purchase. We score these variables and objectively assign points between 0 - 2. The variables are:

1. *Pre-release history*: What did we know about these artists prior to the reviewed albums' release?
2. *Review of three songs* that either charted highest or had a big buzz.

3. *How did it age / does it still sound fresh?* Some albums, cassettes, or CDs in my music collection are best consumed with headphones while a few others are worthy of the window-down-radio-aloud treatment. I could play **Let the Rhythm Hit 'Em** aloud in my car but would keep my enjoyment of **Dana Dane with Fame** private because it did not age as well.
4. *Game-Changer or Pace-Keeper:* Do you remember where you were when you first heard ...? that's the sign of a game-changer. A pace-keeper almost blends with a previous release.

After tallying the scores, the album with the highest overall score is the one we should have purchased first.

Pre-Release History

I have the **Dopeman** album with all those cats bunched up in an alley corner so I approached **Eazy-Duz-It** with some familiarity. At first, I was not quite sure which of the jheri-curled dudes he was, but I did know who NWA was.

Eazy E - 2 points

I heard **Rhyme Pays** and was familiar with "6 in the Mornin'." I also knew Ice T from his cameo in the **Breakin'** movie and could even recite:

> *Once upon a time a DJ's task*
> *Was just to play records, what more could*
>   *you ask?*

CDs, Records, & Tapes

When I arrived in Professional's Record Shop ready to purchase, I already knew who Ice T was.

Ice T - 2 points

Song Reviews

"Boyz-N-The-Hood": in '88, I didn't know what a ghostwriter was. I did know that "Boyz-N-The-Hood" was the best display of lyrics on the album. I thought it was an improvement from "Dopeman." What I would later learn was that I was developing an appreciation for Ice Cube. Nevertheless, I believe this is the best song on the album.

Eazy E - 2 points, 4 total

"I'm Your Pusher" had me hyped from the Curtis Mayfield sample. Even at 13, I understood Ice's play on words. He was using a drug dealer metaphor while consistently discouraging the use of real drugs. His implication was that good music is a better high. A little preachy, but I got it and appreciated the message.

Ice T - 2 points, 4 total

"Eazy-Duz-It" has a humorously catchy beginning followed be bars with which his fans would rap along:

> *Well I'm Eazy-E, I got bi***es galore*
> *You may have a lot of bitches but I got*
>   *much more*
> *Wit my super duper group coming out the chute*
> *Eazy-E, moth******ers, cold knocking the boots.*

I remember the Dr. Dre spliced bridge with Richard Pryor and Kool Moe Dee the most, even co-opting the "where you from fool?" line as a joke among friends.

Eazy E - 2 points, 6 total

"High Rollers" is probably the best example of Ice sharing the story of a hustler while also discouraging participation in the game.

> *Now radio stations probably won't play*
> *This record because of the things I say*
> *They'll say I'm glamorizing the hustling hood*
> *And a record like this can do no good*
> *But I'm not here to tell ya right or wrong*
> *I don't know which side of the law you belong...*

With Ice, it is never a dazzling one-liner, but the context of the larger story that grabs the listener.

Ice T - 2 points, 6 total

"We Want Eazy" was the only track with a video from the album. It shows the group dynamic behind the song and the album. In time, we would see this album as a precursor for **Straight Outta Compton**. A more discerning listener would have noticed by this, the seventh track, that there is not much diversity in content.

Eazy E - 1 point, 7 total

"Personal" stands in for any of the other tracks as an example of Ice as an MC. He's repping LA. He's cool. He understands the game. While respected as a story teller more than an MC, "Personal" shows his MC skills.

Ice T - 2 points, 8 total

How Did It Age?

Power aged better. Back in '88, one of my early impressions was wondering why they (Easy E / NWA) were cursing so much. I had this feeling despite my hometown mayor being known for well-placed curse word. I was also familiar with The Last Poets and Rudy Ray Moore. Yet, even at 13, I thought NWA were just cussing for cussing's sake.

I'll go a step further, while NWA voiced an angst that had not been heard on a national scale (best represented by "F*** the Police"), I would place their biggest consequence was shock value. When comparing them to Ice T, I'll use a move comparison to highlight the difference - I believe Eazy E / NWA are more **Menace To Society** while Ice T is more **Boyz N the Hood** (despite the title being inspired by Eazy's song). **Menace** was shocking and provocative while leaving the viewer with nihilistic hopelessness. **Boyz** addressed the same area, same societal ills, evoked despair, and somehow left the viewer with some hope and some ideas to build upon. I think these distinctions help explain how **Power** aged better than **Eazy-Duz-It**.

Eazy E - 1 point, 8 points
Ice T - 2 points, 10 points

Game-Changer or Pace-Keeper

Eazy-Duz-It was a game changer. Although it was not

the first gangsta rap album, it was the stage-setter for the most well-know gangster rap group. It was the album that bumped Ruthless Records into notoriety.

Power is a pace-keeper. It is a more cohesive album than **Rhyme Pays** and more focused than the subsequent **Iceberg / Freedom of Speech** album; yet, it is consistent with Ice T's modus operendi.

> Eazy E - 2 points, 10 total
> Ice T - 1 point, 11 total

Going back to September 1988, we probably should have bought Ice T first. Actually, I tried to buy the album, but the lady at the record store asked did my mom know I was buying it. So my brother bought the cassette on a different occasion and we played it repeatedly. Same record store, some time later, I bought Eazy E. In the years that have followed, I have listened to **Power** hundreds of times more than **Eazy-Duz-It.**

5

BATTLE OF THE POSSE CUTS: LA VS. THE BAY #1

"I GOT 5 ON IT (REMIX)" VS. "THE GRAND FINALE"

With this Battle of the Posse Cuts, we are swinging it to the West Coast. Keep in mind that these subjective battles follow three rules: competing songs

- Must feature at least three different MCs;
- Cannot be from the same crew; and
- Will be of a similar region.

Since the Oakland team has more MCs, we are going to roll with Dru Down, Numskull, E-40, and Yukmouth for this match-up. Yeah, it's hard to pass up on Shock G and Spice 1, but it is the Luniz's song so we have to include them.

Keep in mind that the battle is scored like a relay. With scoring for each MC scored like this:

- 0 - Maybe y'all should have just sang the hook;
- 1 - Okay, we hear you;
- 2 - Whoa, that was nice!; and
- 3 - DAANNGG, I gotta learn those bars!

Dru Down vs. Ice Cube

Right out the box this is almost unfair. Dru Down embodies some serious Bay Area pride and speaking bad against him doesn't gain me anything. Ice Cube has become an icon. But before he was an icon, he was on "The Grand Finale" and he was just a year or two from being regular ole O'Shea. It isn't far-fetched to say that the 1995 release of "I Got 5 On It (remix)" also catches Dru during his rise as an rapper. So there we go, apples to apples.

For those that don't know, Dru Down and pimping are synonymous. Which is apparent when he opens with:

> *You say you got 5 on my tender, you can bend her over the table*
> *But be sure that you bring my stallion back to my stable.*

If you are unclear with pimp-speak, Dru is informing us that if your money is right, then your sexual needs can be addressed by one of his employees; however, there is a time limit on your escapade. Yeah, that's putting it nicely and glossing over all kind patriarchy and objectification. Yet, this exercise is a study of lyrics and Dru wants us to know he is a pimp. His biggest hits was "Pimp of the Year." See a pattern?

There are some Ice Cube fans who swear by the gospel of Cube. No doubt without him, N.W.A. would have been a group of cussing dudes with great beats. This verse captures that fire that made Cube stand out:

> *Picture a n***a that's raw*
> *Amplify his ass and what you see is what's saw...*

CDs, Records, & Tapes

It was difficult to separate those opening lines from the verse because it all flows so well together. But in this battle, those bars are enough to take this part of the competition.

> Dru Down - 1 / Ice Cube - 3
> "I Got 5 On It (remix)" - 1 / "The Grand Finale" - 3

Numskull vs. MC Ren

Numskull is one of The Luniz and this is a remix of his song - look, I'm not a rapper, but I'll be damned if somebody else gonna outshine me on my track. I'm assuming Numskull felt the same way because he did not re-spit his bars from the original but came with new heat:

> *Cause see, a n***a perpin' broke'll smoke your*
> *   spliff all day*
> *Go home and buy big drinky with his briddy then*
> *   parlay*
> *I got 5 on the Hennessy, Seagram's, or 40's*
> *'Cause "This is How We Do It" like Montell*
> *   Jordan*
> *I'm from the Oakland City, Frank Nitti is a goner*
> *Num' blowing it up like Oklahoma.*

We all recognized that in NWA Ren was overshadowed by Cube. But that does not diminish his skill, Ren was a capable MC. Almost like Charles Oakley, he was not a perennial all-star but you would want him on your team. Ren brought it on when he spit:

> *Giving him pain 'cause I'm urgent*
> *Rearrange their muthafuckin' face like a surgeon*

> *It ain't no excuse for the torture delivering*
> *Don't say you're not scared, yo, I can tell 'cause you're shivering.*

Numskull- 1 / MC Ren - 1
"I Got 5 On It (remix)" - 2 / "The Grand Finale" - 4

E-40 vs. Eazy E

Among the legends that came from the Bay, E-40 stands tall. E-40's unpredictable flow and wordplay will always make him stand out - always. I mean, this is a cat who is "hipper than a hippopotamus " and I don't think you can get hipper than that. However, given the number of MCs on the track, the brothers from The Bay -- "man we gotta get it together!" -- (pardon that Mac Mall shout out).

> *E-40, why you treat me so bad?" 40 makes it happen*
> *Fosgate slappin' and revenue grows*
> *From just a little bit of lightweight flamboastin'*
> *Potent fumes, lingering mighty clouds and Northern Lights.*

Reprinting 40's lyrics does not do him justice because it can't convey his uncanny delivery. The fact that he starts singing in the manner of Club Nouveau's "Why You Treat Me So Bad", the song that was sampled, is indicative of E-40's unusual, witty style.

Whereas Eazy E's "Grand Finale" verse is one of his strongest, you and I know he probably did not write the lyrics. In his verse, he strays toward his sexual exploits, which when considering how he died seems a bit unsettling. Nevertheless, Eazy E sounds well-coached when he said:

> *They made it Eazy for me to come off like the*
> *enforcer*
> *Mass murderin' muthafuckas in a course of*
> *An everyday situation where I would stalk by*
> *Fuck a car, I do a motherfuckin' walk-by*
> *Eazy-E and the D.O. to the C. and*
> *Run house and yo there'll be no disagreeing*
> *'Cause if there is some, you feeling staticky*
> *Then I'm arrested (For what?) assault and*
> *battery.*

Not even Ice Cube's or The D.O.C.'s ghostwriting can offset Eazy's whiny little brother flow. But these are some of Eazy's best bars and it's the closest he'd ever get to E-40.

E-40 - 2 / Eazy E - 2
"I Got 5 On It (remix)" - 4 / "The Grand Finale" - 6

Yukmouth vs. The D.O.C.

Like Numskull, Yukmouth is half of The Luniz and while we got Bay Area legends on the track, Yuk still gotta represent. He does:

> *Me and E-40 to the head, comin' fed plus, you let*
> *the lead bust*
> *Ready to do a murda, mayne; perved off the*
> *Hurricane...*

Forget what you heard from Terrance Howard, when

you hear a cat say, "mayne" - that cat is from The Bay. Between "mayne" and "Hurricane" - a shout out to my favorite track by The Click (E-40, D-Shot, Suga- T and B-Legit), Yukmouth is repping Oakland hard. Yet, at no point in his career, would anyone say that he was lyrically on par with The D.O.C.

One of the biggest 'what ifs' in Hip Hop is what if The D.O.C. had never been in that accident? I think that he would be been a bridge between the macho-gangsta rhyme style commonly then-associated with LA rappers to the more lyrically potent (think: Ras Kass). Dude was nice.

> *But I was smart, the D.O. to the C. knowin' the formula*
> *It's rough, I mean it's funky enough for me*
> *And you can have a listen, helpin' and some dissin'*
> *D-O-N-T M-O-V-E yo without permission*
> *From the D.O. to the C., I'm just better than*
> *The normal man and I'll be damned if a sucker can*
> *Ever compete with the elite, much less speak*
> *It's like dancing with two left feet*
> *Never smile when the Doc is in the room*
> *Or I'mma send ya ass right to the Temple of Doom...*

If Shock G or Spice 1 were running the anchor against The D.O.C. they would have fared better. But things being as they are, we end up with:

Yukmouth - 1 / The D.O.C. - 3
"I Got 5 On It (remix)" - 5 / "The Grand Finale" - 9

Even if we scored all the verses on "I Got 5 On It" I do not think it would have edged the LeBron & Anthony Davis one-two punch of Ice Cube and The D.O.C. "I Got 5 On It (remix)" is designed for thumping your trunk, cooling with your peoples, or getting a little feel good going at the party. "The Grand Finale" is more bravado-battle rap which unfairly tilts this contest toward LA. and Ruthless Records.

6
JUST ONE: SPRING 1990
AMERIKKKA'S MOST WANTED OR LET THE RHYTHM HIT EM'

This match-up is colossal! Two classics that both received 5 mic ratings from **The Source**. Two definitive albums from titans of the culture. The two albums from indisputable Hip Hop legends at the center of this Just One dilemma are Ice Cube's **Amerikkka's Most Wanted** and Eric B & Rakim's **Let the Rhythm Hit 'Em**. This is gonna be good!

We will use 0-2 point scoring system in a couple of categories to help determine which would have been the better initial purchase. The categories are:

1. *Pre-release history*: What did we know about these artists prior to the reviewed albums' release?
2. *Review of three songs* that either charted highest or had a buzz.
3. *How did it age / does it still sound fresh?* Not all of the music in our collection sounds as good today as it did way back when. Seriously, when G.L.O.B.E. does that "ZZZ zzz ZZZ zzz ..." verse in "Planet Rock," my kids look at me with questions.

4. *Game-Changer or Pace-Keeper*: The game-changer will get the nod. For example the first two DMX albums were TIGHT; yet, the whole "where did this dude come from?" astonishment we had when we first heard "Get at Me Dog" separates the first album from the second.

Pre-Release History

Ice Cube was a vital part of NWA and departed just as they achieved national acclaim or notoriety, depending on how you want to look at it. By now, we were well aware that he wrote some of the group's most outstanding verses. However, besides Kawhi Leonard, who leaves a team when they are on top? Ice Cube, that's who.

Ice Cube - 2 points

By this time, Eric B & Rakim were icons. I mean, there are stars. Then there are legends. Then there are icons. With this release, they (particularly Rakim) would ascend to nearly mythological status. We knew these cats very well.

Eric B & Rakim - 2 points

Song Reviews

"The Ni*** You Love To Hate" shows Cube coming out of his corner swinging! At this point, we were accustomed to Cube on a platter of beats by Dre. But the Bomb Squad? At the peak of their game? The "sound" or "vibe" was an assault on the ears - probably just as Cube had planned it. Especially since he was spitting bars like these:

> *Cause I'm about to f**k up the program*
> *Shooting out the window of a drop-top Brougham*
> *When I'm shooting, let's see who drop*
> *The police, the media, and suckers that went*
> *pop...*

Ice Cube - 2 points, 4 total

"In The Ghetto" is my all-time favorite Eric B & Rakim song! In fact, if there was a Hip Hop line that best described me, it would be when Rakim said:

> *I'm so low key that you might not see me*
> *Incognito, and takin' it easy ...*

Oh yeah, this is my joint! Seriously though, I can't think of another MC who can rhyme from the perspective of sperm and take listeners along for the visual ride. Yet, despite having "so much to say ... (he) still flows slow." Consider this - you ain't ever heard of any MC anywhere trying to diss Rakim. Who else has that much juice?

Eric B & Rakim - 2 points, 4 total

"Who's The Mack": it is not often that mellow and Ice Cube go together in the same sentence but on this track the mellow vibe helps facilitate the question of "who's the mack?" or the flip side, who is being played? With different scenarios of cats getting over on people, Cube shifts gears with his flow and nails the track.

Ice Cube - 2 points, 6 total

"Mahogany" was the first time we heard Rakim do a track for the ladies and it is SLAMMIN'! The Al Green sample sets us up for the coolest seduction of a lady in Hip Hop history. Plus, this Rakim, so he went abstract and still brought it home, for example:

> *And soon, you can represent the moon*
> *As long as I keep you in tune*
> *I'll tell you who you are and why you're here*
> *Take it in stride 'cause it might take a year*
> *It's funny - how time flies when you're havin' fun*
> *We got close and it was almost one*
> *She kissed me slow, but you know how far a kiss*
> *   can go*
> *F**k around and miss the show*
> *So I told her to hold that thought real tight*
> *We can finish where we left off later on tonight ...*

Eric B & Rakim - 2 points, 6 total

"Endangered Species": I believe this is a sampling of the Cube that created **Death Certificate**. Communicating the angst of the inner city is different from shouting woof tickets. Add in a guest verse from the legendary Chuck D, and Cube shows he is more intelligent than the shot-em-up, where-the-h**s-at caricatures associated with gangsta rap.

> *You wanna free Africa? I'll stare at ya*
> *Cuz we ain't got it too good in America*
> *I can't fuck with them overseas*
> *My homeboy died over keys ...*

Ice Cube - 2 points, 8 total

"Let the Rhythm Hit 'Em" is showcase of top flight lyrical MCing. You can't help but nudge someone and say "damn, did you hear that?" Back in 1990, I rewound the tape over and over to catch these bars:

> *The prescription's one every hour, now it's a habit*
> *Ya need another hit from the freestyle fanatic*
> *Attention: follow directions, real close*
> *Keep out of reach of children, beware of overdose*
> *Too many milligrams, no one made an iller jam*
> *My rhyme is the rhythm of thoughts that kill*
>   *a man*
> *Ideas for the ear to fear, might split him*
> *He'll never forget 'em, he'll rest in peace with 'em*
> *At least when he left, he'll know what hit him*
> *The last breath of the words of death, was the*
>   *rhythm.*

Wow. I mean, damn. Whoa. Yeah ... whew.

Eric B & Rakim - 2 points, 8 total

How Did It Age?

Back then, we were excited for Cube's debut and he did not let us down. But now, it just sounds like a lot of senseless hollering. Indeed, it captured the frustration of the times and it was true to the gangsta motif Cube represented with NWA. However, now that the times have changed (or have they?), do you feel like listening somebody who ain't never got gaffled like that? **Amerikka's Most ...** deserved the love it got, but sonically, it did not age well.

Let The Rhythm Hit 'Em aged much better. It is a

melodically cohesive album and even three decades later, Rakim's lyrical gems are still prompting "oh sh*t" moments of understanding from listeners. I know I'm playing toward my bias - my preference of later albums over the first. As noted by my preference of OutKast's **ATLiens** over **Southernplayalistic...** or Little Brother's **The Minstrel Show** over **The Listening** and even Cube's **Death Certificate** over **Amerikka's Most ...** - I believe there is a difference from the excitement of a new voice as compared when the artist has really found their voice, their groove. Having said all that, I prefer to listen to **Let the Rhythm Hit 'Em** as an entire album in one setting more than **Paid in Full**.

Nevertheless, **Let the Rhythm Hit 'Em** aged better than **Amerikka's Most ...**

> Ice Cube - 0 points, 8 points
> Eric B & Rakim - 2 point, 10 points

Game-Changer or Pace-Keeper

A West Coast MC with East Coast production? I don't think any of us saw that coming. Despite the fact that Cube was a known commodity, the combination of Cube and the Bomb Squad makes **Amerikkka's Most ...** a game changer.

Let the Rhythm Hit 'Em is an evolution in production. To me, it feels like ideas they tested out production-wise with **Follow the Leader**, were perfected for this album. It is nota game-changer but an evolving, improving pace-keeper

> Ice Cube - 2 points, 10 total
> Eric B & Rakim - 1 point, 11 total

In life, we sometimes wish to right past wrongs.

Knowing what we know now, we would do things differently. I didn't buy either at the moment they dropped but I did buy Cube first. However, knowing what I know now and considering I could only purchase "just one" - I have to go with Eric B & Rakim.

7

COMMON & STEVIE WONDER
PART ONE

When we look at things in hindsight, our view tends to be rosy. With that in mind, these essays will be very rosy. As a lifelong music fan (as an infant, my father baptized me in the waters of musical appreciation with Ahmad Jamal's "Poinciana"), my music collection and roster of favorite artists are vast.

Each morning when I rise, I begin with music. The sounds signal my family that it is time to get the day started. The other morning while I was jamming, I ventured into my Common playlist and my musical appreciation began to brew along with the morning coffee. The brew's final concoction was an idea of paralleling the albums of hip hop artist, Common with musical legend, Stevie Wonder.

To be clear, I know that Stevie Wonder and Common operate to two vastly different levels. In fact, if Stevie Wonder is the Bill Russell of music and Common could very well be Joe Dumars. Bill Russell is considered to be the greatest basketball champion (he coached one championship team while playing on the same team!). Joe Dumars is a Hall-of-Fame basketball player who was such an asset to his team and the game that the NBA Sportsmanship Trophy is named after him. I mention those gentlemen because as remarkable of a basketball player that Joe Dumars was, it is an unfair comparison to compare him to Bill Russell. This piece is not a comparison. It is an appreciation of one artist's discography with the use of an icon's discography as a lens for understanding. Let's get started!

Can I Borrow A Dollar & Music of My Mind

When **Music of My Mind** was released, Stevie was already an established artist. But instead of remaining entrenched in the **Signed, Sealed, Delivered** box of the Motown sound, he had already began to traverse into an unchartered galaxy of melodious creativity. One of the brilliant shooting stars in that galaxy was the 8 minute opus, "Superwoman." This wonderful piece of art also establishes or affirms Stevie's uniqueness when compared to other R&B artists.

It would be a gross stretch to say Common's **Can I Borrow A Dollar** was a comparable artistic statement of uniqueness. Initially, I viewed it as inconsequential and it is the one of two Common albums that I never purchased. That is not an indictment of Common, but instead it is a reflection of where I was in life—a Midwestern teen attending an East Coast HBCU. Common's delivery sounded similar to the East Coast rappers, Das EFX, and much like the Detroit-based rappers A.W.O.L. (who rapped "your wiggity wow wiggity wow is bullsh** to me"), I was defiant in my refusal to embrace any wiggity wiggity rhymes.

My best friend, Jay, didn't share my disdain for wiggity rhymes. In fact, his constant replaying of "Soul By The Pound" caused me to make an exception to my position. I never grew to like that style of rhyming, but I began to think Common Sense (as he was known then) might be alright. Plus, with him being from Chicago, I was willing to have some Midwestern love for him. I wasn't quite a fan at this point, but I had heard enough to set the stage for what would come next. Whereas Stevie's **Music of My Mind** set him apart from other R&B artists, the fact that a Midwest rapper had a national album release and video on Rap City planted the seeds of Common's uniqueness for me.

Resurrection & Talking Book

The stepfather of my friend, John (JV), had the most organized record collection I had ever seen. Albums were organized by genre, alphabetized, and in plastic sleeves. As a child, I handled my parent's records with care because I did not want to get into trouble. But it was through the organization of Wendell's collection that I began to see albums as works of art. It was also through this collection that I came across **Talking Book**. My parents had the album, but as I sat on the couch waiting for JV one day, I paid more attention to the cover art and lyrics on the inside. I also played the album. Within a few days, I knew the whole album by heart. I was an enthusiastic convert to the religion of Stevie-Wonderdom. The despair conveyed on "Blame It On The Sun" resonated in my soul. But that wasn't the album's biggest hit. The most popular song was "Superstition," one of the most iconic songs in American history.

Much like my experience of finally listening to Stevie, I was in a circumstance where I was forced to listen to Common. I was in the car with my friends, Brian and Rashad, and Brian played "I Used To Love H.E.R." and it changed my life! I haven't been the same since. I purchased the cassette and listened to the song well over thousand times that summer. In fact, this was the beginning of my problem of really enjoying the first few tracks of an album and not listening to the rest of the tracks. I think I had the tape for years before I listened to it entirely. While the opening track, "Resurrection," was very good, "I Used to Love H.E.R." is one of the most transcendent hip hop songs of all time. Like **Talking Book**, **Resurrection** is a really good album made historic because it contains a genre-defining, otherworldly hit.

One Day It'll All Make Sense & Fulfillingness First Finale

Some would think that the only thing these albums have in common are their multi-syllablled titles. Yet, I believe they share another similarity. Look at it this way - if Stevie or Common had not recorded any previous or subsequent work, then both of these albums would be more highly acclaimed. In Stevie's case, **Fulfillingness First Finale** is highly celebrated; yet among his acclaimed classic albums (**Innervisions** immediately preceded this album and was not included in this essay), it is the Andrew Bogut of the classic five — the misperceived least important component of a championship starting five. Nevertheless, "Boogie On Reggae Woman" is one of those songs I 'knew' as a child but didn't really understand until I was a man. The same could be said for "Creepin'."

Continuing with the notion that in a vacuum, these albums would be more highly celebrated but because they were sandwiched between Stevie's and Common's more acclaimed work, these albums aren't as celebrated as much as they should be. In Common's case, his most memorable song was released before this album and his next album, well, we will get to that soon. As much as I enjoyed this album, I felt like I was driving a sports car attempting to shift it into a higher gear it didn't have. Again, if **One Day ...** was Common's only album, this essay would be about how slept on he was. "G.O.D." was almost like the thoughts I had during that season of life were recorded by two of my favorite artists (Cee-Lo joins Common on this track). Not only was I wrestling with the limitations of religious practices I experienced as a child, I was also experiencing a full dosage of love relationship challenges. I suppose those challenges (learning how to manage one's admiration, love, and lust) are a part of becoming an adult. While "Retrospect for Life" carries a prominent anti-abortion message, for me it was the background / theme music for learning how to conduct myself with women as a responsible man. The melancholic uncertainty regarding long-term dating during that season of my life matched the undertone of the track. It was in this season that Common evolved from a promising hip hop artist into a legitimate voice within the culture. Common's legitimacy is established and Stevie's is cemented.

8

JUST ONE: APRIL 1990

FEAR OF A BLACK PLANET OR TO THE EAST, BLACKWARDS

The fun in reflecting with these nostalgic essays is revisiting a crucial moment. For this essay, that crucial moment is April 1990 at your local record store. Of all the records, cds, or cassettes on display there, you end up holding one of the following in each hand: Public Enemy's **Fear of a Black** Planet and X Clan's **To the East, Blackwards**. Then there is this - you only have enough money for one. Which do you choose?

We are going to breakdown the choice into a few categories and as objectively as possible, assign points between 0 - 2. The categories are:

1. *Pre-release history*
2. *Review of three song*s
3. *How did it age / does it still sound fresh?*
4. *Game-Changer or Pace-Keeper*

Ultimately, the album with the highest score is the one we probably should have initially purchased.

CDs, Records, & Tapes

Pre-Release History

Public Enemy was at the top of their game. While their first album was okay, their second, **It Takes a Nation of Millions to Hold Us Back**, is one of the most important musical contributions of the last century! It was that monumental. Moreover, "Fight the Power" had been vital to the success of Spike Lee's classic movie, **Do The Right Thing** and was included on this album. PE had a fully steamed locomotive of momentum heading into the release of **Fear of a Black Planet**.

Public Enemy - 2 points

In the spring of 1990, I was 15 years old and I was as about as committed of a Hip Hop fan as one could be. I frequented the record stores in my Detroit neighborhood - Professional's and Chauncey's - and even recorded music videos on VHS so that I could watch them over and over (and at times, horribly replicate the dance steps). Yet, for all of my Hip Hop enthusiasm, I had never heard of the X Clan prior to the moment when I first picked up their album.

X Clan - 1 point

Song Reviews

"Welcome to the Terrordome" is my all-time favorite PE song! My man, Jay, let me hold the cassette single before the album dropped and I played it non-stop. I did the intermittent play - pause - write down the lyrics thing because I was so excitedly energized by the experience. When Chuck said "Every brother ain't a brother cause a black hand squeezed on Malcolm X the man", I had to get my dad to listen to it so that we could talk about that and some of the other lyrics. When my dad heard the song and christened it with "These young brothers is all right" - man, I was proud and became a PE fan for life.

Public Enemy - 2 points, 4 total

"Heed the Word of the Brother": When fans everywhere hear Professor X proclaim "Exist in a state of Vanglorious, as we are protected by the red, the black, and the green, heed the words of the brother ...", they all shout the next word on cue. Then the Parliament sample beat drops and we are introduced to certainly one of the most slept-on MCs ever - the grand verbalizer, funkin' lesson, Brother J! Man, let me tell you, J's consistent, wise, and effortless flow is accentuated by the numerous lyrical gems he dropped. It's been three decades and I still believe "the ever tangled web we weave, always trying to obtain, no attempt to achieve" is one of the most prescient lines ever.

X Clan - 2 points, 3 total

"Fight the Power": It is not an exaggeration to say that this song is historic. In addition to making known our feelings about John Wayne and our displeasure that "most of (our) heroes don't appear on no stamp", this song is energetic and infectious. It deserves to be their signature song and an essential part of Hip Hop history.

Public Enemy - 2 points, 6 total

"Funkin' Lesson" is the first song on the album and it's

smokin'! It's like you give these nearly relatively unknowns a few seconds to make their point and 'ABRACADABRA' they do their thing like it has never been done before. I was riding with my brother, Damon, when we first heard this song. We rewound the tape after the first verse to hear Brother J again. Brother J "walks in the light of the moon, but (he's) never been a Batman, African, call it Black man" Again, his flow amplifies his wordplay.

X Clan - 2 points, 5 total

"Revolutionary Generation" has been an enduringly influential song for me. Prior to hearing it, I do not recall ever hearing an MC take a stand for Black women in the way that PE did with this song. As a writer, my novels focus on healthy portrayals of Black women because I learned from Chuck D - "R E S P E C T, my sisters not my enemy, because we'll be stronger together ..." This is my daughter's favorite PE song.

Public Enemy - 2 points, 8 total

"In The Ways of the Scales" was the first song I played for weeks, each morning as I rose for school. Melodically, it is the perfect cap / end song for this album. Lyrically, when J states "I am an African, I don't wear Greek, must I be reminded of a legendary thief, who tried to make Greece in comparison to Egypt, but they got gypped cause their minds not equipped" - it was just one of the numerous lessons I learned from him.

X Clan - 2 points, 7 total

How Did It Age?

Part of what made Public Enemy so iconic was the uniqueness of their sound. The producers, the Bomb Squad, had these layers of samples that can be discombobulating to virgin ears. Their bombastic sonic confusion allies with adolescent and young adult angst. However, maybe because I'm old, maybe because I'm a parent, I don't know why, but despite my immense love and respect for Public Enemy, nowadays, I can only listen to a few songs at a time. What is essential here is separating nostalgia from present moment. This album fits perfectly in the time in which it was released and musically (not the lyrics or the messages - but the sound), an attribute that made it so unique also impedes it's other timeless qualities.

X Clan sounds like early 90s Hip Hop with its heavy funk samples. Yet, particularly "Raise the Flag", those samples are inspiring, soothing, nostalgically warming. Usually, if I hear one song, I will opt to hear several others.

> Public Enemy - 1 point, 9 points
> X Clan - 2 points, 9 points

Game-Changer or Pace-Keeper

Fear of a Black Planet continues the excellence of **It Takes a Nation of Millions ...** It is a pace-keeper.

> Public Enemy - 1 point, 10 total

To the East, Blackwards was woke before people used the term to shame others. During a time with Afrocentrism was common in Hip Hop, no one represented it to the level

CDs, Records, & Tapes

and quality of X Clan. Moreover, perhaps overlooked, the value of Professor X. Sometimes younger generations shun their elders in a zeal to do things their own way. Considering the machismo prevalent in Hip Hop, X Clan utilized the voice of an elder as a pillar in their production. Years later, Arrested Development would incorporate an elder on a smaller scale; but X Clan in particular and the Blackwatch movement overall felt like a communal experience. It was a game-changer.

X Clan - 2 points, 11 total

Rewind back to Chauncey's Record Shop in northwest Detroit on Evergreen and Six Mile, a 15 year old Sabin Prentis inspected and read the front and backs of the Public Enemy and X Clan albums. I only had enough money for one. Although eventually, I would have both, I know that today I would make the choice just as I did then - I would purchase the X Clan.

9
PUBLIC ENEMY THREE-PEAT
IT TAKES A NATION OF MILLIONS TO HOLD US BACK ~ FEAR OF A BLACK PLANET ~ APOCALYPSE '91

With this Hip-Hop Three-peat entry, we are going to celebrate Hip Hop's second Three-Peat Champions - PUBLIC ENEMY!

"Yes, the rhythm, the rebel!"

To describe Public Enemy as icons is nearly an understatement. As artists, activists, cultural transformers, and more - Chuck D, Flavor Flav, Terminator X, Professor Griff, and the Security of the First World are a multi-faceted and enduring phenomenon.

I will attempt to focus on their artistry as seen through their consecutive classic albums. Consecutive classic albums are a rare feat. Stevie Wonder and Earth, Wind & Fire are two of the most recognizable three-peat (and more) champions in music history. Then Run-DMC proved it could be done with Hip Hop. Which if Run-DMC are the Julius "Dr. J" Erving of Hip Hop Classics, then Public Enemy is definitely the Michael "Air" Jordan of the matter. Yes, it had been done before. And yes, there are similarities in their "game." And yes, the progenitor took the art form up to a higher level.

As seen by the Dr. J - Air Jordan reference (yeah man, I know Dr. J never won three consecutive championships), the NBA bears a heavy influence on this Three-Peat series. As a native Detroiter, it took a long time for me to even begrudgingly cheer for the Bulls (which I didn't until their second three-peat). I continue to harbor feelings of anger regarding my beloved Bad Boy Pistons being robbed in the '88 Finals when Kareem Abdul Jabbar got those free throws because of a foul that never happened. The Bad Boy Pistons went to three straight finals but only won two consecutive championships ('89 & '90). Sort of reminds me of the first three De La Soul albums ... 3 albums, 2 classics. But that's an essay for another day. Let's get back to PE!

FIRST CHAMPIONSHIP - 1988 - IT TAKES A NATION OF MILLIONS TO HOLD US BACK

Where We Were

I own Public Enemy's debut album, **Yo! Bum Rush the Show**. Perhaps it was overshadowed by the immense popularity of LL Cool J's **Bigger and Deffer**. Maybe the dawning of the Golden Age of Hip Hop had not revealed their potential. Maybe, just maybe, that first album was a delightful teaser of what was to come. I believe the latter. All the elements were there, it just hadn't gelled into its' promise.

What made them outstanding

- Chuck D - his cut-through-a-crowd voice and his underrated lyricism;

- They had a fully-developed identity when we met them. They were originals;
- The Bomb Squad had created a multi-layered sound that was as distinctively recognizable as the group itself.

What we could have done without

Not applicable. This album is museum-worthy, college-course-curriculum worthy, and very worthy of every old head telling a youngin' "see this here? This is real Hip Hop."

Championship Moment

The whole thing or to quote John Witherspoon in **Boomerang**, "from the rooter to the tooter!" From the opening track when should have considered ourselves warned until Chuck spits "but it's proven and fact, and it takes a nation of millions to hold us back" on the last song on side two - the whole album is a championship run.

What resonated with me then and now was that it was so distinctive and unlike anything ever heard.

How it impacted me

Let me back up, I got their first album after hearing their second. **A Nation of Millions ...** was so good I need more immediately. Most importantly, what I learned from PE or they compelled me to learn. I eventually read Assata because Chuck D said: "recorded and ordered, supporter of Chesimard." Or not only did they bring John Coltrane to my awareness, the notion of a certain caliber of purposeful artistry being interconnected struck me when Chuck said:

CDs, Records, & Tapes

> *The book of the new school rap game*
> *Writers treat me like Coltrane, insane*
> *Yes to them, but to me I'm a different kind*
> *We're brothers of the same mind, unblind*
> *Caught in the middle and not surrendering*
> *I don't rhyme for the sake of riddling.*

To me, he establishes his uniqueness while connecting it to a larger narrative. Prior to 1988, such a concept was beyond my grasp. But thanks to PE, I not only "got it", I aim to live it.

SECOND CHAMPIONSHIP - 1990 - FEAR OF A BLACK PLANET

Where We Were

I really believe the table was set when "Fight the Power" became the anthem for the summer of '89 and a vital component of Spike Lee's **Do The Right Thing**. Add that atop the serious momentum or reverberations from **A Nation of Millions ...** and the time was ripe for something monumental.

What made them outstanding

- How do you top a classic? With another one!
- Simultaneously maintained what made **A Nation of Millions...** great while evolving their sound and message;
- A stellar example of addressing social issues, promoting cultural pride & awareness, and innovating sound - a masterful artistic

accomplishment.

What we could have done without

Again - not applicable.

Championship Moment

I may be alone with this sentiment - if I had to introduce Public Enemy to someone who did not know them, I would play "Welcome to the Terrordome." Yes, PE has a trunkful of hits. Was "Fight the Power" a hit because of it's exposure through the movie? Ehhh, to a degree. But "Welcome to the Terrordome" definitively marked their evolved sound from **A Nation of Millions ...** and whetted my appetite for more!

How it impacted me

I was fifteen when the album dropped and I began my preparations for school by playing the sequence of songs on side two ("Who Stole the Soul"- "Fear of a Black Planet" - "Revolutionary Generation"). Not only was I ready to face the day, I felt wiser and more empowered. Sometimes, I wish I could have captured that magic in a bottle.

THIRD CHAMPIONSHIP - 1991 - **APOCALYPSE 91 ... THE ENEMY STRIKES BLACK**

Where We Were

I'm going to revisit the Bad Boy Pistons. I alluded to them being robbed of what should have been the '88 championship. Yet, what I will honestly acknowledge is that by that second (should have been third) championship they were showing wear. The Pistons posted one of the worse regular season win-loss totals of any NBA champion and PE, while wining the third championship, was also showing ... wear? fatigue? the last vestiges of the closing Golden Age?

What made them outstanding

- Important messaging in the lyrics - nowadays folks like to shame and say such lyrics are "preachy." Despite his authoritative voice, I never found Chuck D to be "preachy." Instead, I heard that his message was important;
- "Nighttrain" is the best song on the album. I love the beat breakdown in between the verses - man that's perfect! Plus, true to their modus opendi, PE teaches through their rhymes and on "Nighttrain" we really get the message that "all skin folks ain't kinfolks ..."

You musn't just put your trust in every
  brother, yo
Some don't give a damn, cause they the
  other man
Worse than a bomb, posin' as Uncle Toms
Disgracin' the race, and blowin' up the
  whole crew
With some of them lookin' just like you.

- Courage - they could have stayed in their comfort zone, but NOOOO they hit us with relevant perspective on contemporary topics. This differs from 'Important Messages' as that covers what they said, this point acknowledges the fact that they would even say it all.

What we could have done without

This feels sacrilegious, like saying your grandmother's roasted turkey is dry. But in all fairness, the momentum slows on side two.

Championship Moment

Being provocative with "By the time I Get to Arizona" through both the song and video. "Can't Truss It" was a valuable history lesson. "By the time ..." was a (then) current issue. PE would not play it safe and they proved it with this song.

How it impacted me

Apocalypse 91 dropped at the beginning of my senior year in high school and side one of the cassette was on regular rotation. Yet, just as the last year of high school signals the end of an era, so does **Apocalypse 91**. But if you focus on the ending, you miss the lessons that are in play and **Apocalypse 91** is full of lessons.

Championship Reflection

Public Enemy still releases new music. My last PE purchase was **How Do You Sell Soul To A Soulless People Who Sold Their Soul?!** and it's lyrical punch and value was vintage PE. I guess it's like the one teacher in high school or college that really opened your eyes to learning. You thrived

CDs, Records, & Tapes

in their class and eventually moved on. Perhaps you have been so moved to visit your old school and see them still doing their thing (shoutout to HU's Professor Robert Watson!). That's PE for me - at a highly impressionable time, they infused my spirit with history, confidence, and a sound that matched my adolescent angst. I'm glad they are still doing their thing and I am eternally grateful for their historic three-peat that blessed my life immensely.

10

BATTLE OF THE POSSE CUTS: COAST-TO-COAST

"SELF DESTRUCTION" VS. "WE'RE ALL IN THE SAME GANG"

There aren't many songs in Hip Hop that embody "posse cuts" more than these two. I can only think of one, Ice T's "What You Wanna Do?" But these two, they are much more widely known. On one hand, the artists were taking a public stand against violence and on the other hand, uniquely representing their region. Almost like an East Coast vs. West Coast rap battle without the declaration of not having a producer all up in the videos.

By now, you know these battles are subjective and follow three rules. The competing songs:

- Must feature at least three different MCs;
- Cannot be from the same crew; and
- Will be from a similar region (the Hip Hop nation is the region).

Additionally, the battles are also scored like a relay:

- 0 - Maybe y'all should have just sang the hook;
- 1 - Okay, we hear you;

- 2 - Whoa, that was nice!; and
- 3 - DAANNGG, I gotta learn those bars!

And like a relay, we need to whittle this all-star team down to four representatives: KRS-One, Kool Moe Dee, MC Lyte, and Chuck D (with Flavor's ad-libs) vs. King Tee, Above the Law, Digital Underground, and Eazy E

KRS-One vs. King Tee

Truly, this is just my opinion; yet, it seemed to me that the Stop the Violence Movement was a real thing while the West Coast All-Stars was in response to the popularity of "Self-Destruction." The catalyst of the Stop The Violence Movement is the Blast Master KRS-One, who sets the table with:

> *"Well, today's topic, self destruction*
> *It really ain't the rap audience that's bugging*
> *It's one or two suckers, ignorant brothers*
> *Trying to rob and steal from one another*
> *You get caught in the mid*
> *So to crush the stereotype here's what we did*
> *We got ourselves together*
> *So that you could unite and fight for what's*
>   *right."*

Whereas King Tee opens with:

> *It's straight up madness everywhere I look*
> *Used to be a straight a student, now he's a crook*
> *Robbing people just to smoke or shoot up*
> *Used to have a crew cut, now he's a pooh-butt*

> *Dropped out of school and he joins the*
>   *neighborhood gang*
> *Hanging on the streets selling 'caine*
> *To his own people*
> *Now when I say people I mean color*
> *You a stupid mother-*

More legendary than his verse is the effort and vision KRS-One had to exert to make this historical milestone happen. Yet, with both MCs, they are simply setting us up for what to expect.

KRS One - 1 / King Tee - 1
Stop The Violence Movement- 1 / West Coast All - Stars - 1

Kool Moe Dee vs. Above the Law

One challenge with posse cuts is maintaining the uniqueness of one's voice. I think in some cases, voices become blended into one hodgepodge of a song. The best MCs standout amid the crowd, just like Kool Moe Dee:

> *Took a brother's life with a knife as his wife*
> *Cried 'cause he died a trifling death*
> *When he left his very last breath*
> *Was "I slept so watch your step"*
> *Back in the sixties our brothers and sisters were*
>   *hanged*
> *How could you gang-bang?*
> *I never ever ran from the Ku Klux Klan*
> *And I shouldn't have to run from a black man.*

When it comes to Ruthless Records, Above the Law was

my favorite group. That favoritism influences this review because until they spit, I really wasn't feeling the song:

> *Bein' the pimps that we are*
> *We're here to speak on a situation that has gone*
>   *too far*
> *Here at home in the ghettos of LA*
> *Where a young black brother's not promised to*
>   *see the next day*
> *Cause we used to clock on the streets before we*
>   *made beats*
> *But fools just lay and prey on the weak*
> *It don't depend on the color of a rag*
> *Cause if you got what they want you know they*
>   *gonna take what you have*
> *Cause violence don't only revolve from drugs and*
>   *thugs*
> *And gangs that bang*
> *Most times it's a political thang...*

This could be a pretty interesting match-up as both of these artist sort of peaked in popularity before their respective coasts blew up. Nevertheless, as far as these tracks go:

Kool Moe Dee - 2 / Above the Law - 2
Stop The Violence Movement- 3 / West Coast All - Stars - 3

MC Lyte vs. Digital Underground

Lyte not only adds feminine flavor, but her unique voice allows her to follow Kool Moe Dee without missing a beat:

> *Funky fresh dressed to impress, ready to party*

> *Money in your pocket, dying to move your body*
> *To get inside you paid the whole ten dollars*
> *Scotch taped with a razor blade taped to your*
> > *collar*
> *Leave the guns and the crack and the knives alone*
> *MC Lyte's on the microphone*
> *Bum rushing and pushing, snatching and taxing*
> *I cram to understand why brothers don't be*
> > *maxing*
> *There's only one disco, they'll close one more*
> *You ain't guarding the door, so what you got a*
> > *gun for?*
> *Do you rob the rich and give to the poor?*

Yet, not even the lovely Lyte can top the interplay between Shock G and Humpty Hump:

> *I'm in a rage*
> *Oh yeah? Yo, why is that G?*
> *Other races, they say we act like rats in a cage*
> *I tried to argue, but check it, every night in*
> > *the news*
> *We prove them suckers right and I got the blues*
> *America*
> *Get busy, Humpty*
> *The red, the white, the blue and*
> *The blue and the red*
> *For Crips and Bloods*
> *The white for who's got you doin*
> *Time bustin caps on one another*
> *The Underground's down for peace among*
> > *brothers.*

The beat breakdown during the song enhances Digital Underground's verse and gives them the edge against Lyte.

MC Lyte - 2 / Digital Underground - 3
Stop The Violence Movement- 5 / West Coast All - Stars - 6

Chuck D & Flavor Flav vs. Eazy E

No contest. Yeah, their legends for their respective reasons. On one hand, it's easy to underestimate Chuck's flow because his voice is so outstanding. Flavor is the perfect compliment and they work their magic here:

> *Yes, we urge to merge, we live for the love of our*
> *people*
> *The hope: they get along (Yeah, so we did a song)*
> *Getting the point to our brothers and sisters*
> *Who don't know the time (Boyyyee, so we wrote*
> *a rhyme)*
> *Instead in your head, you know, our job*
> *To build and collect ourselves with intellect*
> *(Come on)*
> *To revolve, to evolve to self-respect*
> *'Cause we got to keep ourselves in check*
> *Or else it's..."*

The perfect end to that song. Now Eazy seeks to stay hard on a stop the violence track - go figure:

> *Last but not least, yo, Eazy's no sell-out*
> *And if you can't hang in the streets, then get the*
> *hell out*
> *I'm not tryin to tell ya what to do*

> *You have your own freedom of choice who to*
> *   listen to*
> *You knew good from bad, fair from foul, right*
> *   from wrong*
> *Now your mother's singing that sad song*
> *(My baby ain't never hurt nobody!)*
> *But he still got smoked at BeBe's party*
> *But you're not the first or the last*
> *You're nothin but a short story from the past*
> *You're dead now, not number one but a zero*
> *Take notes from Eazy-E, the violent hero.*

Chuck D & Flavor Flav - 3 / Eazy E - 1
Stop The Violence Movement- 8 / West Coast All - Stars - 7

The Stop the Violence Movement is the champ!

11

JUST ONE: OCTOBER 1992
WHUT? THEE ALBUM OR CAN I BORROW A DOLLAR?

By October 1992, I had been in college for a couple of weeks and was beginning to appreciate the musical taste of my roommate, Rashad. Initially, we both had reservations. He was a fan of the Fu-Schnickens and the UMCs while I was a believer in the Poison Clan and Detroit's Most Wanted. But Rashad had a subscription to **The Source** and could easily identify a random jazz sample in a Hip Hop track, so my initial reservations began to thaw. Then he introduced me to Redman and Common Sense.

Which leads to our moment of truth between Redman's **Whut? Thee Album** and Common Sense' **Can I Borrow a Dollar?**. If you were like Rashad and I, funds were limited, so splurging on two cassettes was not only a gamble but an infringement on your laundry money. However, like we've done with previous installments, we are going to use a 0-2 point scoring system in a few categories to help us with our choice. The categories are:

1. *Pre-release history*
2. *Review of three songs*

3. *How did it age / does it still sound fresh?*
4. *Game-Changer or Pace-Keeper*

Pre-Release History

Rashad played EPMD's "HeadBanger" ad nauseam. But I endured it because I liked EPMD and thought K-Solo was cool. Watching Rashad enthusiastically recite each line was hilarious particularly when he did a Damon Wayan's Handyman type dance when Redman said that line about cerebral palsy - pure comedy. Heading into his release, I was well aware of who Redman was.

Redman - 2 points

I never heard of the rapper we know as Common but who was then Common Sense. When Rashad played the tape, that was my first time hearing from him.

Common - 1 point

Song Reviews

"Time 4 Sum Aksion" was instant energy! Rashad was jumping all over the room. Moreover, that was the first time I heard "straight outta Jersey!!" It would become a popularly shouted refrain all around campus. We even had a cat tagging dorms with "Straight Outta Jersey." Yep, Redman was so infectious he turn college kids to graffiti artists.

Redman - 2 points, 4 total

"Take it EZ": I was excited for a rapper from the

Midwest getting some national attention. I liked the beat and found myself saying "oh sh**" recalling the memories prompted by his lines (Sha-na-na-na and "I gots the Magic but I'm not a Laker"). The damper on my enthusiasm was my opinion of his flow which was seemingly inspired by Das EFX (which I disliked). Nevertheless, I was rolling with this cat.

Common Sense - 2 points, 3 total

"Blow Your Mind" - you guessed it, Rashad's antics reached an enthusiastic pitch when this came on - "AAAAAHHHHHHHHHH!! LOOK OUT!" I could follow the Gap Band sample more clearly than Red's flow. I was like, 'how does he say all that in one breath?' BUT, I did press rewind to get my mind blowed (again).

Redman - 2 points, 6 total

"Breaker 1/9": this comment is definitely one made in hindsight to explain the unease I had with Common Sense - he sounds like a promising rapper who hadn't found his voice yet. His wit was evident. The rhyme skills were promising and the beats were dope. Yet, then and definitely now, the Das EFX flow? I'm glad that time has passed.

Common Sense - 1 point, 4 total

"Tonight's Da Night" had me going. I was thinking this dude about to be smooth with it. Then Hurricane G cuts in and gets him back to his regular wild self. In shading Common Sense on the wiggity flow, I can also hear its' influence on Redman. Yet, at this stage of their careers, I could hear a greater distinction or uniqueness in Reggie's flow more than I could with Common.

Redman - 2 points, 8 total

"Soul by the Pound": just for the record - the remix bangs tougher than the album version. All my comments are the same - I hear the potential, like the beats, but not the flow.

Common Sense - 1 point, 5 total

How Did It Age?

Common was tremendously better by his sophomore album, the classic, **Resurrection**. In some ways, **Can I Borrow ...** is to Common what **Words from the Genius** is to the GZA - a nearly forgettable debut from an artist who became exceptional. **Can I Borrow...** did not age well.

Whut?! Thee Album aged better while still sounding dated. It was with this album that I started to appreciate Erick Sermon as a producer.

So does it come down to No I.D. or Erick Sermon? Somewhat, in both cases the beats matched the times. But the uniqueness of Redman's flow and style carries him here.

Redman - 2 points, 10 points
Common Sense - 1 point, 6 points

Game-Changer or Pace-Keeper

A midwestern MC with a national release? I can't say I recall that happening. I was purchasing a number of local acts or Rap-A-Lot or Bay Area rappers from the mom & pop record stores. But Common was on Rap City; he deserves some love there.

Whut?! Thee Album was better than EPMD's **Business Never Personal** album which is unique because how often does the guy who got put on have an album better than the guy who put him on? Okay, Jay-Z over Jaz-O. Name another ... now looking back on a whole body of work, folks will say Royce outshines Em but technically they are peers so it doesn't really fit. Point being, Redman was a game-changer because you had not experienced an MC like him.

> Redman - 2 points, 12 total
> Common Sense - 2 points, 8 total

Not even close.

I am a Common fan. I own (read: paid money for) ten of his twelve albums but I never purchased **Can I Borrow...** Actually, I don't remember when Rashad purchased it either, it seems like at some point in time he just had it. I vividly remember him purchasing Redman and eventually **Whut?** is the only Redman album I would own. Which brings us back to this match-up. Redman was the purchase we should have made back in October 1992.

12

COMMON & STEVIE WONDER
PART TWO

In the first installment, I introduced the notion of using Stevie Wonder's albums as a lens for viewing Common's albums. In no way is it meant to be a comparison as much as it is an effort to enjoy two artists' music at one time. We've covered the first three albums, so let's pick-up at:

Like Water for Chocolate & Songs In The Key of Life

Some of the purists would debate others as to whether **Like Water for Chocolate** is better than **Be**. The older-school purists would debate whether **Songs In The Key of Life** is better than **Innervisions**. All of them would be correct because all of those albums are classics. These two in particular are the albums that make-up a chunk of arguments when fans begin bantering back and forth about the best songs.

Songs In the Key of Life has so many hits, if someone wasn't familiar with it already, they would assume that it was a greatest hits compilation. I believe this album pushed Stevie onto the icon plateau. "As" and "Knocks Me Off My

Fee"t stand out; yet, if forced to choose, "Love's in Need of Love Today" gets my vote for it's timeless.

Like Water For Chocolate featured JDilla backing Common with the beats. I have to confess that even as a Detroit dude, I was late on the Dilla bandwagon. My tardiness to Dilla is the scarlett letter on my Hip Hop fandom. But this is the album that made me a fan. DJ Premier certainly did his thing with "The 6th Sense," but when the album hits with "Nag Champa" and "Thelonious" back-to-back? Things got hella real right there. Those joints are the ones that you bump in the ride when you are riding with your guys. But when you are with your lady? That's the time to bump "The Light."

With these albums, both artists cranked their creativity up to a higher gear. Both albums are like treasure chests of golden musical memories. It is nearly impossible to listen to either and not scrunch up your face and say "Hell Yeah!" With **Like Water for Chocolate**, Common delivered his first classic album and Stevie did some Steph Curry magic by following an MVP-caliber album (**Innervisions**) with something even more off the chart. Arguments that these represent the high water mark for both artists could be pretty sound. No one would question the logic. However, we all know that it's impossible to remain at the mountain's peak.

Electric Circus & Journey Through The Secret Life of Plants

More than one fan listened to these albums and asked, "What in the hell?" I know I did. While some fans wondered what Stevie and Common were trying to prove, both albums proved that they weren't just entertainers, they are artists.

Authentic artist take risk. They do not conform to what's

popular; instead, they innovate. With these albums, both brothers were in full innovation mode.

Truthfully, what dulled my initial experience is I approached both albums with biases. With Common, I was unfairly expecting **Like Water For Chocolate** part 2 and with **The Secret Life of the Plants**, I was expecting ... well, hell ... I don't know what I was expecting but I wasn't expecting what I heard. However, I grew to appreciate the artistic risk and with time liked both **Electric Circus** and **The Secret Life of Plants** more than I did at first.

For those who longed for the Stevie with whom they were familiar, "Send One Your Love" is the track for them. On an album loaded with instrumentals, the lyrics of 'Send One..." easily reminds listeners of Stevie's stellar songwriting (in this case I'm referring to lyrics. He is also a magnificent melodic composer).

"Come Close" was the leading single from **Electric Circus** and possible moved Common from a meager crush to starring role in the dreams of many women. For the brothers, I think "Aquarius" serves the lyrical punch we come to expect from Common. In fact, as I listened to the album more, it grew on me with each listen. While it is not my favorite Common album, I believe a lot of the resistance against it was unmerited. Probably from people who rely on soundbites for information when real knowledge comes from research. Critics of **Electric Circus** should revisit the album, its' formidable value may surprise them.

Be & Hotter Than July

Legendary boxer Roy Jones, Jr., succinctly summarizes the mistakes of fair-weather fans when he rapped, "Y'all Must Have Forgot!" Those who thought the musically

CDs, Records, & Tapes

artistic explorations of Common and Stevie meant their skills had diminished, must have forgot. The heaping helpings of soul contained on both these albums would certainly have helped them remember.

Hotter Than July contains one of the most frequently sung choruses in "Happy Birthday." You know what I mean, that time when a handful of people gather to sing the traditional "Happy Birthday" song and the one or two who try to be hip and they sing it Stevie's way. The other people are less cool and slow to catch-on while messing up the rhythm. Then after the chorus is looped four or five times, everyone looks around like, "What do we sing next?" One person tries to keep it going but really the mood has been soured because Stevie's classic has been desecrated for cheap thrills. Man, I hate when that happens!

Nevertheless, if folks did forget about Stevie's genius, **Hotter Than July** does more than reminds them; it makes one of the most compelling cases in music history. Even today, nearly forty years later, one way to get the party started is to kick-off with "All I Do." If you're feeling like a love relationship didn't go your way, then there is "Rocket Love." Suspicious that your lover has another? Then there is "Lately." Someone trying to come at you with BS, let them know "I Ain't Gonna Stand For It." With this album, Stevie covers a wide terrain of emotional matters.

With **Be**, Common delivers a knockout!! I believe it is his masterpiece, slightly edging **Like Water For Chocolate** only in its' concise efficiency. When those stand-up bass strings are strung on the opening track, that is the jab setting up the knockout punch that is "The Corner." The lyrical artistry of "The Corner" made me replay it multiple times before moving forward. Then I had to "GO!" Truthfully, I drove the long way home so that I could listen to the CD repeatedly. I remember contemplating buying a new car and carried this cd from car to car to discern how well the sound systems were. There is a hypothetical scenario that people pose that goes like this: your house is on fire and you can only save a few cds, which do you grab? **Be** is one of the must-grabs for me.

No earnest listener of **Be** can overlook the infectious rhythm of "They Say." If they try, we will say that "they don't know!" But we know that Common is an amazing artist capable of producing Hip Hop classics.

13

JUST ONE: NOVEMBER 1993

MIDNIGHT MARAUDERS OR ENTER THE WU-TANG

Picture this: it's November 1993 and you have just enough ends to purchase one CD or cassette. You are in your favorite record store and faced with a choice that wouldn't be easy even 30 years later. The choice was between A Tribe Called Quest's **Midnight Marauders** or the Wu-Tang Clan's **Enter the Wu-Tang (36 Chambers)**.

To helps, we will assign 0-2 points in these categories:

1. *Pre-release history*
2. *Review of three songs*
3. *How did it age / does it still sound fresh?*
4. *Game-Changer or Pace-Keeper*

The album with the highest score is the one we should have initially purchased.

Pre-Release History

ATCQ was coming off their successful second album, **Low End Theory**, and had taken monumental creative strides since Tip left his wallet in El Segundo. The jazz samples of **Low End Theory** made me a sure fan where I had once been casual. **Midnight Marauders** dropped early in my sophomore year at Hampton University and the buzz was crazy! It wasn't just East Coast cats or backpackers anticipating this release, we all were anxious to see if they could build on the success of **Low End Theory**.

ATCQ - 2 points

I'm not sure any of us was ready for Wu-Tang when they dropped. The first single, "Protect Ya Neck" had already dropped but was making a gradual rise from the underground. I first heard the Wu at a party when everyone sang the bridge of "Method Man" - you remember? When he had the phat bags of skunk, the White Owl blunts, the forty, and the shorty? But not even that prepared me for the seismic shift in the Hip Hop landscape that was **Enter the Wu-Tang**. But for folks beyond Shaolin and the Tri-State area, it probably seemed like the Wu came out of nowhere. There was not precedent or much like the inspiration for one of the clan's names, their style had no father.

Wu-Tang - 1 point

Song Reviews

"Award Tour": The first five seconds? That rhythmic melody? Fans were hooked from get-go. Looking back, I recognized that Phife's lyrics usually struck me as soon as I heard them but Tip's rhymes sort of snuck up on me and I caught the cleverness a little later. Either way, whether you chose to "do that do that do that that that" or "take your garbage to St. Elsewhere" - you knew when you heard "Award Tour" that there would be no letdown from their previous album.

ATCQ - 2 points, 4 total

"Protect Ya Neck": Man, what in the entire hell? C'mon, you ain't never ever hear anything like Protect Ya Neck before. I'm sure I wasn't the only one confused. In fact, I didn't really get it until I heard it in the context of the whole album. After that? I got it. The kung-fu, the lack of chorus, an array of distinctive respectable MCs? Yeah, it was a lot at first but eventually I would get hype and "swing through your town like your neighborhood Spiiiiiiider-Man."

Wu-Tang - 1 point, 2 total

"Electric Relaxation": My all-time favorite ATCQ track! The beat is CRAZY!! "Honey check it out you got me mesmerized, with you black hair and yo phat - a** thighs" is a visual that would mesmerize many of us.

ATCQ - 2 points, 6 total

"C.R.E.A.M." is more than a song - it's a flag-planting, chest thumping, sonic declaration that "WE ARE HERE!" This joint is damn near a movement by itself! When the beat drops and Raekwon spits "I grew up on the crime side, the New York Times Side, stayin' alive was no jive" - even the non-believers had to accept the truth that the Wu-Tang Clan wasn't nuthin' to F with!

Wu-Tang - 2 points, 4 total

"Oh My God" - well, let's just say since "Electric Relaxation" was the high point for me, "Oh My God" was the descent down from the top. Still good music. Same fresh vibe. But after those first two singles? The momentum slowed a tad.

ATCQ - 1 point, 7 total

"Can It All Be So Simple" was my favorite track on the album. I'm predisposed to soul music and the laid back vibe of this song helped me "hear" the Wu. Plus, it really started to sink-in that despite the variety of MCs, there was no drop off in rhyme quality. I didn't hear this until I listened to the whole album. Everybody was shouting about what ruled everything around them but for me, it was so simple to get attached to this song.

Wu-Tang - 2 points, 6 total

How Did It Age?

I listen to different music genres and have a jazz music collection that would make your grandfather jealous. My love for melodies makes me consider Tribe. Then again, I'm also an artist who creates with words and I have a strong respect for originality and reinvention. The backstory of how Prince Rakeem became the RZA or the future lesson of how they negotiated solo deals for everyone are pillars in the WU mythology.

Yet, when considering how these albums aged, I'll go here with it: if a random track popped up on your music shuffle playlist - how likely are you to listen or skip? With that as a factor, I go with Tribe. Lyrically, this is like Clash of

CDs, Records, & Tapes

the Titans; so the discerning factor for me are the beats or the music. You almost have to be in a particular mood for the Wu, while you can vibe to Tribe in different moods.

Too close to score

Game-Changer or Pace-Keeper

Midnight Marauders is the two in the one-two punch that is ATCQ second and third albums. In that light, it's a pace-keeper.

ATCQ - 1 point, 8 total

Enter the Wu-Tang was like a lightening bolt on a sunny day - it came with tremendous power out of nowhere. It's a game-changer.

Wu-Tang - 2 points, 8 total

Back to the record store via November 1993 - had you picked either one, you would have purchased a winner.

14

A TRIBE CALLED QUEST THREE-PEAT

PEOPLE'S INSTINCTIVE TRAVELS AND THE PATHS OF
RHYTHM ~ THE LOW END THEORY ~ MIDNIGHT MARAUDERS

With our third Hip-Hop Three-peat entry, we are going to dive into perhaps the first group that came to many minds when we introduced this notion of Hip Hop Three-Peats – A Tribe Called Quest. Throughout this series, I have referenced the inspiration of NBA Three-peat Champions in helping recognize the higher echelon of extraordinary performance that is required to release three consecutive classic albums. I won't say that Tribe is Jordan's Bulls and their two three-peats but the Shaq & Kobe three-peat Lakers come to mind. I could draw some parallels, but would rather not – let's get into these championships!

FIRST CHAMPIONSHIP –1990 - PEOPLE'S INSTINCTIVE TRAVELS AND THE PATHS OF RHYTHM

Where We Were

In 1990, we were enjoying the barrage of quality music that was turning this time into Hip Hop's Golden Age. From Eric B & Rakim, Big Daddy Kane, and even NWA – we were getting bombarded with classic after classic. Just when things could not get any better, one of four peculiarly dressed artists left his wallet in El Segundo.

What made them outstanding

- Dispelling assumptions – I was guilty. The quick glance assumption made me (and probably a few others) think these guys were De La knockoffs. WRONG. They were original with their primary connection to De La being their choice to stand apart from everyone else. These cats were authentic from the jump.
- Stickiness – their songs were catchy, nearly infectious as listeners would find themselves, rapping, humming, or otherwise replaying Tribe's songs in their head after the initial listening experience.
- Their sound – beyond the lyrics, their beats were distinctive. Lyrically with what they said and how they delivered their words, they expanded on their distinctiveness. There was something about these guys that had listeners feeling like "you gotta put me on."

What we could have done without

This is tricky because hindsight could have us getting real nit-picky. But recalling the context of 1990 and the fact that this group seemingly came out of nowhere (for many listeners) – this album is a remarkable introduction to a new group. We needed every bit of this album.

Championship Moment

I believe this extends beyond 1990. The championship moment is enduring because even for late-coming Tribe fans, revisiting this album is a joy. It aged very-well. Among the highlights, I found "Can I Kick It?" to be sort of a beacon to where they were headed and I was anxious for the ride.

How it impacted me

In 1990, I was in the tenth grade and concerned with the height and flatness of my hightop fade. I liked "El Segundo" but it was "Bonita Applebum" that made me a fan. Even right now, when you read these lyrics:

> *38-24-37 (mmm, mmm, mmm)*
> *You and me, hun, we're a match made in heaven.*

a happy feeling and/or memory takes over your mind. Only a classic song has that type of impact.

SECOND CHAMPIONSHIP – 1991 - **THE LOW END THEORY**

Where We Were

It was the start of our senior year of high school and I had worn out Ed O.G. & Da Bulldogs' **Life of a Kid in the Ghetto** and King Sun's **Righteous but Ruthless**. We were ready for something new. My man, Jay, copped the "Check the Rhime" cassette single and we played it non-stop while getting more and more amped for the album.

What made them outstanding

- More Phife! Want to make a good team great? Increase the input from a talented teammate.
- Their sound jumped up several notches in uniqueness. For some old heads, when the notion of jazz and Hip Hop come up, they think of the late Guru from Gangstarr. Guru was indeed that dude; yet, for me, all jazz and Hip Hop talk leads to Q-Tip (with a shoutout to Jazzy Jeff and the "Touch of Jazz").
- The imagery – they evolved from bohemians into regular cats. But more important than that? The Afrocentric-theme lady mascot is iconic!

What we could have done without

Not applicable – **The Low End Theory** is perfect.

Championship Moment

"Scenario" is the best posse cut of all-time! The video was ground-breaking. Phife and Tip shined and Busta Rhymes' guest verse is classic. Moreover, with this album Phife's line about himself is also prophetic for the group:

> *My days of paying dues are over, acknowledge me as in there.*

How it impacted me

I was a fan but I was not a hardcore, ride-or-die fan. In all honesty, my growing love of jazz music, particularly the jazz fusion era, made me revisit **The Low End Theory** with a different ear and different anticipation. I love it more now than I did in '91. Not that it wasn't deserving of the love then, but I was not as sophisticated of a listener to really appreciate those samples and beats. In '91, I thought the album was very good; however, as an adult, I know this joint is a classic.

THIRD CHAMPIONSHIP – 1993 - **MIDNIGHT MARAUDERS**

Where We Were

Dr. Dre's **The Chronic** had changed Hip Hop. Particularly catapulting the West Coast to the top of Hip Hop popularity. While I never heard of Tribe getting involved with that East vs. West nonsense, I believe that the release of **Midnight Marauders** and the Wu-Tang's **Enter the Wu-Tang (36 Chambers)** definitely started shifting the momentum back East. Their joint releases perhaps kickstarted the birth of the "second" Golden Age.

What made them outstanding

- "Electric Relaxation" – my favorite Tribe track!
- Good – better – best progression we saw with Run DMC's Three-peat is also evident with Tribe's Three-Peat with **Midnight Marauders** being best of their classics.
- The album cover – not only did fans think they were dope, but other artists and producers also wanted to be down with their iconic group. Plus, the Afrocentric-themed lady was back!

What we could have done without

Perfect – it's an album you can listen to again and again.

Championship Moment

That euphoric moment when you realized that it doesn't get better than this. For some of us, the flip side of that thought was the realization that it wouldn't.

How it impacted me

As a sophomore from the Midwest at a college on the East Coast, I was standing rigid in my unimpressed-with-East-Coast-rappers position. Really, it was just adolescent defiance. I was homesick for the rappers with whom I was most familiar while gaining an albeit begrudging appreciation for new music coming from the East.

On the day Midnight Marauders dropped, I was at a rehearsal for a production our forensics team was putting together. My classmate, Willita, was from New Jersey and damn near had the album memorized by our rehearsal that evening. She would not stop saying "Do that, do that, do that, that, that" throughout rehearsal. I tried to be annoyed but then she let me listen to "Award Tour" and I was infected with her enthusiasm.

Championship Reflection

The passing of Phife casts a somber pall over my Tribe memories. The loss of an artist with whom we grew-up is a reminder of our mortality. The differences that existed among the group members is a reminder of the ebbs and flows of our childhood friendships. The music that they sampled was a reminder that our music stands on the shoulders of those who came before us.

These dudes were game-changers. They are the soundtrack of some of my fondest memories. Moreover, their last album, **We Got It from Here... Thank You 4 Your Service** is very good and is a fitting capstone to their discography. Whenever you want to recapture the magic of your youth, press play on track 9 of **The Low End Theory**, then do those punches in the air with each of those "unh, unh, unh (s)" and ... well take it from there:

> *Back in the days on the boulevard of Linden*
> *We used to kick routines and the presence was*
> *fittin'...*

15

JUST ONE: APRIL 1994
ILLMATIC VS. SOUTHERNPLAYALISTICADILLACMUZIK

If you've been with us on this ride of nostalgic essays, then you know the central premise is this: you're in the record store during a specific moment in time and you only have enough money for one purchase. Today, the moment is April 1994 and the difficult choice involves Nas' **Illmatic** and OutKast' **Southernplayalisticadillacmuzik**. The memories of which makes me shout "WOO!" like Ric Flair.

To determine which we should have purchased first, we will assign 0-2 points in the following categories:

1. *Pre-release history*
2. *Review of three songs*
3. *How did it age / does it still sound fresh?*
4. *Game-Changer or Pace-Keeper*

Pre-Release History

Nasty Nas had a serious buzz due to his appearance on the Main Source's "Live at the BBQ" and the anticipation was intense. In hindsight, I supposed it is fair to say Nas was an underground MC – "underground" implying lyrical skill over commercialized packaging. Some would envision him as some sort-of Luke Skywalker taking the (Hip Hop) Empire back from the West Coast. However you saw him, the pending release of Illmatic had madd hype.

Nas- 2 points

I first experienced OutKast through the video for "Player's Ball." Immediately, I pictured me and man, Jay, cruisin' Jefferson Ave and Belle Isle. More than any other Hip Hop group, I felt a kinship, a relatability, a bond with OutKast. I bought the cassette single that day and was not deterred by its Christmas theme. These were going to be my guys. Their contribution to the LaFace compilation album generated buzz heading into the release of their first album.

OutKast – 2 points

Song Reviews

"Life's A B****" was the first song I played for my birthday every year from 1994 - 2016. If you were to bottle-up some Hip Hop, tossed it into the sea, and some stranger on an isolated island opened and heard AZ talking about "visualizing the realism in life and actuality" – they would be hooked. AZ's verse is one of the greatest in Hip Hop history. But this is about Nas, right? He delivers too. His "I woke up early on my born day" was the impetus behind my annual birthday listen as I turned 20 in 1994. In some ways, this song is a mainstay in my young adulthood soundtrack.

Nas – 2 points, 4 total

"Player's Ball": In seeing myself through OutKast, I am particularly speaking about the artist we would eventually know as Andre 3000. I saw Jay as Big Boi. Over time, we have come to know Dre for some off the wall stuff while Big Boi has been consistently down-to-Earth and in touch with their core audience. In '94, they were almost interchangeable. Their voices wouldn't be more distinctive until their second album, **ATLiens**. Nevertheless, Dre's notion of "having made it through another year, can't ask for nuthin' much mo'" fit my view of navigating late adolescence.

OutKast – 2 points, 4 total

"The World is Yours": This was the first song I heard from Nas and I was gone. In '94, I was still entrenched in my biases and blindly committed myself to any Hip Hop that wasn't from New York. Nas changed that and broke down those bullshit barriers I had erected. My college friends, Brian, Ed & Trev staged an intervention and the song that changed my position was "The World is Yours."

> *I'm the young city bandit,*
> *Hold myself down single-handed,*
> *For murder raps, I kick my thoughts alone,*
> *Get remanded, born alone, die alone,*
> *No crew to keep my crown or throne,*
> *I'm deep by sound alone, caved inside,*
> *1,000 miles from home.*

The Ahmad Jamal sample was the icing on the cake.

Nas – 2 points, 6 total

"Git Up, Git Out": if we are going to talk about AZ's spotlight-stealing bars, then we must also mention Cee-Lo's scene-stealing on "Git Up, Git Out." His thick Southern drawl accentuates the potency of

> *I don't recall, ev'a graudatin' at all,*
> *Sometimes I feel like I'm just a disappointment to*
> *y'all.*

Yep, he stole the show despite Big Gipp, Dre, and Big Boi's good verses. Moreover – and I keep coming to this – the song captures the frustration of young adulthood for African American males within or in proximity to poverty. It's an awkward space: the comfort zone of the familiar and the pending reality of having to make a go at life on your own. Add in racism and other societal ills and life becomes a treacherous landscape to traverse. Through the music I was able to commiserate with others, like when Dre said:

> *I should've listened when my mama told me,*
> *That, if you play now, you gonna suffer later,*
> *Figured she was talking yang yang so I payed her*
> *no attention,*
> *And kept missing the point she tried to poke me*
> *with,*
> *The doper that I get, the more I'm feeling broke as*
> *s***.*

OutKast – 2 points, 6 total

"It Ain't Hard To Tell": to me, listening to an album is a singular experience. Singles are cool and repeats of certain songs is expected, but as a music fan the whole listening experience of the album is my greatest expression of fandom. "It Ain't Hard To Tell" is the last song on the tape and it's the perfect closer. I think these lines capture the essence of Nas:

> *This rhythmatic explosion, is what your frame of*
> *   mind has chosen,*
> *I'll leave your brain stimulated, ni***s is frozen,*
> *Speak with criminal slang, begin like a violin, end*
> *   like Leviathan,*
> *It's deep? Well, let me try again.*

Yep, classic Nas bars that flow and then make listeners pause to think of the magnitude of what he said.

Nas – 2 points, 8 total

"Crumblin' Erb": let me be clear, the best listening experience for "Crumblin' Erb" includes Big Rube's "True Dat" (the preceding song on the tape). Big Rube sets the stage and Dre and Big Boi definitely deliver. I reflect on the summer of 1994 as the last summer of irresponsibility and I specifically recall being posted up on Jefferson Ave with Jay and Mike playing this song again and again. The Marvin Gaye sample along with Sleepy Brown on the hook made this my favorite track on the album.

OutKast – 2 points, 8 total

How Did It Age?

If these albums were to come over your speakers now, how many tracks would be skipped? This is where Illmatic's efficiency stands apart. Although I believe PA from the Dungeon Family released an album prior to **Southernplayalistic...**, there is a feeling that this album represented the introduction of the whole Dungeon Family. Which lends it an expansiveness and breadth that while memorable, lends the listening experience some excess fluff. I truly say that in hindsight because in '94, Peaches doing to the intro was important. Whereas now that OutKast are established icons, we don't need to be introduced to them or Atlanta. Going back to the idea of these albums playing right now – I honestly believe that both you and I would listen to a greater percentage of **Illmatic**'s 10 tracks than **Southernplayalistic..**'s 17 tracks.

> Nas – 2 points, 10 points total
> OutKast – 1 point, 9 points total

Game-Changer or Pace-Keeper

Both were game-changers – it wasn't "hard to tell" that the "South had something to say!"

> Nas – 2 points, 12 total
> OutKast – 2 points, 11 total

Rewind back to 1994, where a soon-to-be 20 year Sabin Prentis was in the throes of the broke college student years. I made it through the summer with homemade dub tapes. Those tapes had songs from both artists. I wouldn't actually purchase **Southernplayalistic...** until after **ATLiens**; however, I did finally gathered enough coins to purchase the **Illmatic** cassette – which then like now, rightfully fits as the initial purchase between these two.

16

BATTLE OF THE POSSE CUTS: NEW YORK EDITION

"24 HOURS TO LIVE" VS. "TRIUMPH"

The Battle of the Posse Cuts brings it back to the East Coast via 1997 featuring two of the most popular teams in the game at that time: Bad Boy Records and the Wu-Tang Clan! While "24 Hours to Live" is indeed the kind of track we have in mind when we discuss "posse cuts", the styles and personalities within the Wu are so diverse any track with them is a posse cut.

Note that for this battle, we went in order, one-for-one matching MCs and then went with the closer. Which means the GZA, Masta Killa, and Ghostface will sit this one out.

These battles follow three rules:

- Must feature at least three different MCs;
- Cannot be from the same crew; and
- Will be from a similar region.

Also note, that the battle is scored like a relay with each MC being scored this way:

- 0 - Maybe y'all should have just sang the hook;

- 1 - Okay, we hear you;
- 2 - Whoa, that was nice!; and
- 3 - DAANNGG, I gotta learn those bars!

Puff Daddy vs. Ol' Dirty Bastard

I won't score these introductions but want to use them to highlight the profound differences between to the two teams. Amazingly, Bad Boy Records had some momentum following the assassination of the Notorious B.I.G. Ma$e's **Harlem World** was the label's next big release and "24 Hours to Live" is featured on it and is the antithesis of the shiny suit extravagance for which Bad Boy was becoming known.

We would be hard pressed to find a more distinct opposite of shiny suits than the Wu-Tang in particular and ODB, specifically. The expensive budget that went into the "Triumph" video is more of a testimony to how popular the group had become and certainly not an attempt by them to be jiggy. Nevertheless, the contrast between Puff and ODB set the table for colossal match-up.

Ma$e vs. Inspectah Deck

It's pretty accurate to say that Ma$e was at his peak in 1997. But peak-Ma$e wouldn't want it with Inspectah Deck even if it was Inspectah Deck's worse day. At one time, Ma$e was Murda Mase and perhaps that was his position when he spit:

> *I'd do good shit like take kids from the ghetto*
> *Show them what they could have if they never settle*

Take every white kid from high class level
*Show 'em what Christmas like growin' up in the
    ghetto.*

Um, yeah, okay. But when you take bars like that and match them up against bars like this:

*I bomb atomically, Socrates' philosophies and
    hypotheses
Can't define how I be dropping these mockeries.*

It seems so very, very unfair. Inspectah Deck's opening is like a boxer's first jab being a Mike Tyson haymaker to the jaw. The type of blow that would make a man search for a new religion.

Ma$e - 0 / Inspectah Deck - 3
"24 Hours to Live" - 0 / "Triumph" - 3

Jadakiss vs. Method Man

This hurts because Jada is one of my favorites. Even my kids recognize Jada's flow and can recite some of his rhymes. But with all the love I got for Jada, Jadakiss on this track is like that last year when Tracy McGrady was on the Toronto Raptors. You could see dude was going to be a monster while you could also see he hadn't quite locked it down yet.

*Yo, yo if I had twenty four hours to kick the
    bucket, f**k it
I'd probably eat some fried chicken and drink a
    Nantucket
Then go get a jar from Branson*

> *And make sure I leave my mother the money to take care of grandson.*

Part of what makes Jada remarkable is his flow and his voice. But if voices help anyone standout, then the voice of the M-E-T-H-O-D Man is certainly a prime example.

I'm going to say this right now as a confessional - when I first heard the Wu's first joint, "Protect Ya' Neck," I was confused. It was just too much going on. In my Kevin Hart voice, "I wasn't ready." So like the immature teen-ager I was, I misunderstood the opening shot from a group that would change Hip Hop in numerous ways. Yet, amid my overwhelmed confusion with "Protect Ya' Neck," I did recognize the uniqueness of Method Man's voice. Fast forward to "Triumph" and I wasn't confused any more:

> *As the world turns, I spread like germ*
> *Bless the globe with the pestilence, the hard-*
> *headed never learn*
> *This my testament to those burned*
> *Play my position in the game of life standing firm*
> *On foreign land jump the gun out the frying pan*
> *Into the fire, transform into the Ghost Rider*
> *A six-pack and A Streetcar Named Desire ...*

The years following 1997 would show Jadakiss coming into his own. But in this match-up?

Jadakiss - 2 / Method Man - 3
"24 Hours to Live" - 2 / "Triumph" - 6

Black Rob vs. Cappadonna

In '97, Black Rob's "Whoa" had not been released yet, thus making this the first time I heard him on wax. While his lyrics fit the vibe of the song, there is an underlying anger that sounds foreboding.

> *Then I'm off to get choke and smoke one of them dreads*
> *And get that b***h from '89 that gave us up to the feds*
> *Thought of momma, wrote her a note, we ain't close*
> *I hate her boyfriend so I put one in his throat*
> *Fuck around and sniff an ounce of raw, bust the four*
> *Pause, pull out my d*** and take a piss on the floor.*

While growing to appreciate the Wu, I was a little lost on Cappadonna. Then I heard "Winter Warz" and knew dude could bring it. On "Triumph" he goes:

> *Vocabulary 'Donna talking, tell your story walking*
> *Take cover kid, what? Run for your brother, kid*
> *Run for your team and your six-can't-rhyme groupies*
> *So I can squeeze with the advantage and get wasted*
> *My deadly notes reign supreme, your thought is basic ...*

Closest head-to-head so far. Cappadonna is on a legendary track with legendary MCs, but I can't say these are his most legendary bars. Black Rob's bars really feel like a warning from a MC on the wrong record label.

> Black Rob - 1 / Cappadonna - 1
> "24 Hours to Live" - 3 / "Triumph" - 7

Sheek Louch vs. U-God

Sheek ain't no slouch. I think initially, he did not stand out as much as Jadakiss, but Sheek can spit. However, much like Jada on this track, he hadn't come into his own as a MC but he does provide a little payback for those who crossed him:

> *What hey yo, if I had 24 n***a gotta get the raw*
> *Run all them papis' spot, put one in his head at the door*
> *For the times that I paid for twenty and he gave me twelve*
> *The other eight had to be baking soda by itself.*

If Sheek and U-God have anything in common, it is that they are overlooked within their respective groups. But the gap between U-God and his WU brethren is bigger than the gap between Sheek and the rest of the Lox. U-God is like Clyde Drexler on the Dream Team. Yes, he deserves to be there; yet, he is surrounded by generational talents. Nevertheless, he spits on "Triumph":

> *Olympic torch flaming, we burn so sweet*
> *The thrill of victory, the agony of defeat*
> *We crush slow, flaming deluxe slow for*

Judgment Day cometh, conquer, it's war
Allow us to escape Hell, globe spinning bomb
Pocket full of shells out the sky Golden Arms.

Well ... let's move on.

Sheek Louch - 1 / U-God - 2
"24 Hours to Live" - 4 / "Triumph" - 9

Styles P vs. RZA

It's starting feel like a blowout. I mean without B.I.G., Bad Boy was missing a preeminent MC and listening to The Lox sounds like these dudes had not yet reached their potential (or maybe they were out of place and why their escape to Ruff Ryder was necessary). But the Wu were in their prime, like Jordan & the Bulls with six championships or classic albums under their belt. Speaking of which, since we're all up in 1997 - let's take the Chicago Bulls thing a step further. That year, they swept a promising Washington Bullets team in the first round of the playoffs (which could mean Jadakiss is Chris Webber and Styles P is Juwan Howard). Alright, I'm going too far - back to the rhymes. Styles P continues with the fatalistic killing sprees when he raps:

If I had 24 hours to live, I'd probably die on the
 fifth
Run in the station squeezin' the inf'
I'll be waitin' to get to hell and bust down Satan
Styles on this shit and I got spot vacant
Back to the 24 I make it out the precinct
Shootin' n****s that I hate in they face while they
 eatin'.

Then we get the RZA. To borrow an analogy used by sportswriters - RZA is on the Mount Rushmore for Hip Hop Businessmen with Jay-Z, Master P, and J Prince. He would even be on the Mount Rushmore for Hip Hop Producers with Dr. Dre, DJ Premier, and JDilla - but okay, back to the rhymes. With all his talents, RZA sounds uncomfortable as an MC. Like his flow doesn't flow. As irksome as his delivery was on this track, his lyrics provided a snapshot of his wisdom.

> *March of the wooden soldiers, C-Cypher-Punks couldn't hold us*
> *A thousand men rushing in, not one n***a was sober*
> *Perpendicular to the square we stay in gold like Flair*
> *Escape from your dragon's lair ...*

Yep, it's the Bulls vs. Bullets all over again.

Styles P - 1 / RZA - 2
"24 Hours to Live" - 5 / "Triumph" - 11

DMX vs. Raekwon

OH SH*T! This some John Cena vs. Shawn Michaels wrestling match-up level competition right here!

"24 Hours to Live" dropped months before DMX's classic, "Get At Me Dog" - hold up, can't acknowledge "Get At Me Dog" without a GRRRRRRRRR, ARF ARF!! DMX's verse here has a similar about-to-blow intensity:

> *24 left until my death*

*So I'm gonna waste a lot of lives, but I'll cherish
    every breath
I know exactly where I'm goin', but I'mma send
    you there first
And with the shit that I'll be doin', I'mma send
    you there worse
I've been livin' with a curse, and now it's all about
    to end
But before I go, say hello to my little friend
But I gots to make it right, reconcile with my
    mother
Try to explain to my son, tell my girl I love her
C-4 up under the coat, snatch up my dog
Turn like three buildings on Wall Street, into
    a fog
Out with a bang, you will remember my name
I wanted to live forever, but this wasn't fame.*

X was sending cats to Hell (and back). I can't say these are his best bars, but they totally end the track with a bang. Speaking of ending with a bang, as noted earlier, we skipped over a few MCs to balance out this relay. "Triumph" went from the RZA to the GZA to Masta Killa to Ghostface and then Raekwon - yep, the hits just kept on coming. It's fitting that the track ends with Ghost and Rae because the synergy they showed on "Fish" and "Verbal Intercourse" almost makes those cats an iconic duo within an iconic group - like Steph and Klay on the Golden State Warriors. Rae spits:

*Hey yo that's amazing, gun in your mouth talk,
    verbal foul off
Connect thoughts to make my man Shai walk*

> *Swift notarizer, Wu-Tang, all up in the high-riser*
> *New York Yank visor, world tranquilizer*
> *Just the dosage, delegate my Clan with explosives*
> *While, my pen blow lines ferocious*
> *Mediterranean, see ya, the number one traffic*
> *Sit down the beat God, then delegate the God to see God*
> *The swift chancellor, flex, the white-gold tarantula*
> *Track truck diesel, play the weed God, substantiala*
> *Max mostly, undivided, then slide it, it's sickening*
> *Guaranteed, mad em jump like Rod Strickland.*

Only Raekwon as the linguistic dexterity to make all that flow. That verse in uniquely Rae; just as X's verse is uniquely DMX. No winner here, it's a tie.

DMX - 2 / Raekwon - 2
"24 Hours to Live" - 7 / "Triumph" - 13

One more basketball analogy before we wrap up - back in the day when the Magic, Bird, & Jordan Dream Team was prepping for the Olympics, they played the college all-stars. A number of those college all-stars went on to have impressive NBA careers. But during that match-up, they were no match for the Wu-Tang Clan, oops, I meant the Dream Team.

17
BATTLE OF THE POSSE CUTS: MIDWEST EDITION
"THUGGISH, RUGGISH BONE" VS. "PO' PIMP"

YESSIR! The Battle of the Posse Cuts stops by the Midwest! As a native of Detroit, my Midwest pride is strong. So strong that my hometown pride for local rap groups like A.W.O.L. and Detroit Most Wanted made me, for a time, a reluctant fan of some other voices in Hip Hop. My Detroit-ness slowed my appreciation for Das EFX or Blahzay Blahzay. However, interventions from my main man, Rashad, in the form of his incessant replaying of Redman expanded my listening palate. "Po' Pimp" and "Thuggish Ruggish Bone" were my efforts to help Rashad appreciate the Midwest.

These battles follow three rules:

- Must feature at least three different MCs;
- Cannot be from the same crew; and
- Will be of a similar region.

Also note, that the battle is scored like a relay with each MC being scored this way:

- 0 – Maybe y'all should have just sang the hook;
- 1 – Okay, we hear you;
- 2 – Whoa, that was nice!; and
- 3 – DAANNGG, I gotta learn those bars!

Notes: this match-up will feature three MCs from each track. Wish Bone will sit this one out only because he had the shortest verse. Also, Do or Die and BONE are established groups; yet, the guest appearance of Twista and the diversity within BONE allow me to make this small concession. Trust me, you have to listen to a lot of BONE to be able to distinguish their uniqueness.

Layzie Bone vs. AK-47

I'm guessing that there is a rap manual somewhere that says: "With your first track, you have to let the people know who you are." Although BONE had an underground EP prior to the release of "Thuggish Ruggish", this is when they make their first national statement. Layzie's intensity and fire lays down the gauntlet from the jump, Cleveland is here!

> *You're feelin' the strength of the rump, step up*
> *Hear the funk of the jump that the thugstas feel*
> *Just be thuggin', straight buzzin'*
> *Lovin' your peoples cause we so real*
> *Chill, better bring your weapon when steppin'*
> *Bring on that ammunition, trip and don't slip*
> *Not to mention, never knew no competition...*

The written word doesn't capture his angst, but trust me, BONE came out swinging.

Swinging isn't what comes to mind when AK starts;

smooth would be more fitting. It's almost like this match-up features some hungry Cleveland underdogs going up against some laid-back Chicago players. Both groups use a rapid-fire and harmonizing rhyme style. However, if you've ever seen **The Mack**, then when I say Do or Die's harmony evokes Goldie's linguistic style, you understand.

> *It was seven double-oh P.M*
> *Fly low to them hoes in the B-M*
> *Sipping Seagram, chewing on a weed stem*
> *Touching on my fo' fif*
> *Move it to the back so I can see who beeping this*
> *Po Pimp...*

AK personifies the unfazed, cooler-than-a-fan, pimp persona. It's almost like this rap thing is no thing because he got this other thing, you know what I mean? But Layzie, he's hungry and it shows. First relay leg goes to:

Layzie Bone - 2 / AK-47 - 1
"Thuggish Ruggish" - 2 / "Po' Pimp" - 1

Krayzie Bone vs. Belo

FLOW is the name of this battle and for me, Krayzie's flow is the easiest to recognize in BONE as he tends to be the one with the most harmonizing within his flow (pun intended). So while his lyrics are cool, if you tried to deliver them as he did, you would be tongue-tied:

> *Now follow me, now, roll, stroll off deep in*
> *the Land*
> *We'll creep if you can*

> *Take another swig to the brain, rose*
> *Loc'in, steady chokin' off that potent smoke*
> *And running from the po-po ...*

Of all my favorite Hip Hop tracks, I do the most mumbling when trying to rhyme with BONE (and I know I'm not the only one). Singing along as opposed to mumbling along is what sets Belo apart. All "Po' Pimp" fans would rhyme along on cue when he said:

> *Mmm, ain't this some sh**, pull up in the C-A*
> *D-I, double-L, pumping A-C, A see hoes*
> *They peep those, P-I, M-P, and they think that*
>   *automatically*
> *Cause he's a pimp, he gotta be full of that*
> *M-O, N-E, but why*

With Krayzie there is a "you-can't-rhyme-like-is" thing going. With Belo, the singalong is catchy and makes his verse a communal experience for fans. Neither is breaking new ground with content matter so that leaves us with this outcome for the second leg:

Krayzie Bone - 2 / Belo - 2
"Thuggish Ruggish" - 4 / "Po' Pimp" - 3

Shatasha vs. Johnny P

Nope, neither of them rhyme on the track. They both sing the intros, hooks, and outros. In many ways, their contributions helped make these songs big hits. I wasn't the only signing:

> *"It's the Thuggish Ruggish*
> *Bbbooooooooonnnnneeee"*

Or

> *"Do you want to rrrriiiiiiddddee in the backseat of*
> *a Caddy, chop it up with Do or Die?"*

Slight nod to Shatasha for name-dropping the whole team, herself and letting us know Cleveland was definitely in the house.

Shatasha - 2 / Johnny P - 2
"Thuggish Ruggish" - 6 / "Po' Pimp" - 5

Bizzy Bone vs. Twista

The significance of flow has already been emphasized. Bizzy comes with a rat-a-tat-tat fire and Twista – formerly known as Tung Twista, who considering his standing in the Guinness Book of World Records, might be the originator or at least, a preeminent early pioneer of the rapid syllable flow. Bizzy came out, guns- blazing with:

> *Gotta give it on up to the Glock-Gock*
> *Pop-pop, better drop when them buckshot, blow!*
> *The Bone in me never no hoe, so*
> *No creepin' up outta the Ziplock...*

Point made. Yet, for all those who do the rapid-fire flow, what makes Twista the king of that thing is that he does not lose enunciation with speed. You may not be able to say what he said as fast as he said it, but you can clearly understand what he said and that my friend, is no small feat. In "Po' Pimp," he sticks to the subject matter and steals the spotlight from Do or Die (which is perhaps why he was the closer). Really, the lyrics are little too graphic to quote at length but we can just start with this:

> *Well, a motherf***er might be broke and sh***
> *And then collecting no dough from tips*
> *But I be spitting mo' game than a mouthful of*
>   *poker chips"*
> *"Spitting more game than a mouth full of poker*
>   *chips?*

Yep, dude spitting crazy game. In addition to his flow, the wit and "oh-that's-what-he-meant", takes Twista's verse up another notch.

Bizzy - 1 / Twista - 2
"Thuggish Ruggish" - 7 / "Po' Pimp" - 7

A tie – can you believe that? Would Wish Bone's verse be a difference maker? I don't know. But I do know both of these tracks were major when they dropped. Oddly, I'm actually more partial to Chopped & Screwed remixes of Do or Die tracks than the originals. Also, I think I speak for all of us when I say we could not have predicted how HUGE "Tha Crossroads" would be for BONE. It was such a big hit that it explains how, in hindsight, BONE became much more significantly well-known than Do or Die. But in terms of lyrical skills on their respective first national releases? BONE and Do or Die earn a tie.

18
COMMON & STEVIE WONDER
PART THREE

If you've been following along, you know that this is unique take on Common's albums through the lens of Stevie Wonder's albums. It isn't a comparison; yet, it is quite simply one way to enjoy two artists' music in one forum.

Finding Forever & In Square Circle

I have never created an album of music and I have certainly never blessed the ears of the world with a classic album. So my credentials for the following comments should be taken with a humongous grain of salt. With that considered, Public Enemy's **A Nation of Million To Hold Us Back** and *F*ear of a Black Planet are so sonically similar that they feel as though they were created in the same recording sessions. As it relates to Common, *Finding Forever* is not the knockout punch that *Be* was; instead it is a win by points on the scorecard.

The last Stevie Wonder album covered in this series, **Hotter Than July**, is a classic or like Common's **Be**, a knockout. Also comparable to Common's **Finding Forever**, **In Square Circle** is a scorecard winner.

Both albums contain singles that are mandatory inclusions in conversations about Common's & Stevie's best songs. "The People" was one of the songs I used to introduce my children to Hip Hop (I would rhyme along while driving and when I got to the part where he says, "my daughter found Nemo" both of my girls would rock excitedly in their baby seats).

It would be inaccurate to say "Overjoyed" is slept-on, but I seldom see it on any of Stevie Wonder greatest hits albums. More than likely it is due to the expansiveness of Stevie's catalog. But "Overjoyed" always stood out to me. It (along with LL Cool J's "I Want You") was one of the first songs where I actually copied the lyrics down verbatim. Even as a ten-year old, I thought the song was enticingly poetic. I was also hoping that I could compose a love letter that was equally enchanting. I wasn't too successful with that letter. In fact, I opted to impress the girl by riding on the bumper of the school van. Truly, a terrible idea and instead of impressing the girl, I busted my nose on the taillight. The scar remains etched over the bridge of my nose. I probably would have been more successful giving her my handwritten lyrics to "Overjoyed."

If I were to produce an album, one track would build out from the instrumental breakdown at the 4:00 minute mark of "Forever Begins." It segues perfectly into Pop's Rap and caps the album.

Universal Mind Control & Characters

Perhaps you may recall the music video for MC Hammer's "Turn This Mutha Out." There is a moment in

CDs, Records, & Tapes

the beginning when some random dude is like "Hammer! You ain't hitting in New York, so what you gonna do about that HAMmer?!" I imagine someone is like "PRENTIS! You defended **Electric Circus,** but what you gonna say about **Universal Mind Control**?!"

I can't say a thing. This is the one outlier that messes-up my little experiment. In retrospect, when I didn't buy the cd in the first few weeks of its' release should have been a clue. I eventually copped it from the bargain bin at the resale shop. I got madd respect for Common, so I made sense of this album by viewing it as artistic experimentation. The vibe made me feel as if I were some college rave party. It felt like when your good friend is dating an unattractive person. He is still your guy and because you got good history, you just sort of give him a pass. Common has enough credibility with me to get a pass.

With Stevie's **Characters,** it is apparent that the golden era ended with **Hotter Than July**. His genius shines through on "You Will Know." While all knew that the glory days had passed, we also knew a post-glory days Stevie is still more engaging than a great percentage of singers and songwriters. "You Will Know" is one of those songs that you forgot you liked. But when you hear it, it conjures a certain calm that only the greatest of songwriters can convey. Another song from **Characters** you may have forgotten about was "Skeletons." Stevie took us to church with this one. All in all, it is a better outing for Stevie than **Universal Mind Control** was for Common.

19

JUST ONE: FEBRUARY 1996
ALL EYEZ ON ME OR THE SCORE

I am an avid rooter for the underdog. Sometimes, I'm right, like when picked Kawhi's Raptors over Embid's 76ers. Sometimes, I'm wrong, like picking the Fab Five to beat Duke. But nevertheless, I won't let my love for the underdog lead to scenarios that are downright foolish. For example, doing a Just One essay matching any artist up against **The Chronic** or **A Nation of Millions** .... To paraphrase Ghostface, it's some "sh** you just don't do!"

However, not all sacred cows are so sacred. Few artist provoke more blind irrationality than Tupac. Bring up Tupac and folks get all up in their feelings. True, he is an icon and was tragically taken from us too soon; but sentiment won't allow me to say he was the best MC / lyricist in Hip Hop history because that ain't true.

Today, we're going to challenge one of Hip Hop big dawgs, Tupac, with a group you may have heard of - The Fugees. Both **All Eyez On Me** and **The Score** dropped on the same day (shout out to my man, Malik for pointing that out) and we're going to use our scoring categories to determine which of the two you should have purchased first. The categories are:

1. *Pre-release history*
2. *Review of three songs*
3. *How did it age / does it still sound fresh?*
4. *Game-Changer or Pace-Keeper*

Pre-Release History

Allow me to state my bias, I think **Me Against the World** is Tupac's best album. But whichever album you may deem as the best, there is no denying that in February 1996, Mr. Shakur was well known to Hip Hop heads coast-to-coast.

2Pac - 2 points

The Fugees visited my alma mater to promote both their albums. I didn't really get into **Blunted on Reality** but when I got a chance to usher their concert with Groove Theory, George Clinton, and a then unknown Maxwell (I saw his warm-up but don't know why he didn't perform) - I thought I had died and went to heaven. Particularly having the fortune to see Lauryn Hill up close, I couldn't think of a better angel than that. For a band looking to better their debut album, The Fugees had a buzz that was building.

The Fugees - 2 points

Song Reviews

"California Love": I can't think of a song I'm tired of hearing more than this one. BUT when it dropped?

Coupled with the fact most folks didn't know Pac was out of prison? Man, it was MAJOR. I won't go into much detail about the type of club I was in when I first heard the song but the performances from that night align some pretty captivating memories with the song. Yet, I mentioned being tired of hearing this because it got so much airplay. I got older relatives that sing Roger Troutman's part during the family reunion. Needless to say, it was a mega-hit.

2 Pac - 2 points, 4 total

"Fu-Gee-La": At first, I didn't think the Teena Marie loop was going to work. But I underestimated Wyclef's magic and the hypnotic siren Lauren proved to be. It was nowhere near as big as "California Love" but it was a significant upgrade over their first album. Clef was right when he said, "We used to be number 10, now we're permanent at one."

The Fugees - 2 points, 4 total

"2 of Americaz Most Wanted": 2Pac and Snoop is a better combination than Harden and Westbrook. Yep, I mentioned those two because at first it seems like they won't fit, but DJ Quik put his thing down on the production and they delivered a classic.

> *So now they got us laced*
> *Two multi-millionaire motherf****rs catchin'*
>   *cases*
> *Bi***es get ready for the throw down, the s**t's*
>   *about to go down*
> *Me and Snoop about to clown*

*I'm losin' my religion, I'm vicious on these stool
   pigeons
You might be deep in this game, but you got the
   rules missin'
N***as be actin' like they savage, they out to get
   the cabbage
I've got nothin' but love for my n***as livin'
   lavish...*

2Pac - 2 points, 6 total

"Killing Me Softly" is probably the bonafide hit that made a very good album great. It feels like Hip Hop although it's definitely R&B. I'm not sure how much you know about Roberta Flack, but it is damn near sacrilegious to attempt to remake one of her songs. But they did and knocked this joint out the park! "One time, one time."

The Fugees - 2 points, 6 total

"Ambitionz As A Ridah": Hands down, my wife's favorite 2Pac song (mine is Picture Me Rollin'- which I will cover in Battle of the Posse Cuts). This is her go-to track for testing out any sound system. Additionally, when we're doing a long family road trip and it's her turn to take the wheel, all of us are awakened by her enthusiastic recital of

*I won't deny it, I'm a straight ridah
You don't wanna f**k with me ...*

It is a flag-planting declaration for starting an album.

2Pac - 2 points, 8 total

"Ready or Not": Lauryn Hill is a dope MC. Not a dope female MC, but a dope MC, period. Check out this rhyme:

> *I play my enemies like a game of chess*
> *Where I rest, no stress, if you don't smoke sess*
> *Lest I must confess, my destiny's manifest*
> *In some Gor-tex & sweats, I make tracks like I'm*
>   *homeless*
> *Rap orgies with Porgy and Bess*
> *Capture your bounty, like Elliot Ness, yes ...*

The Fugees - 2 points, 8 total

How Did It Age?

Both of these albums capture a moment of time quite possibly because they defined that moment in time. In some ways, **All Eyez on Me** was the capstone or one of the last big album to a era that was coming to a close. **The Score** was a harbinger of what was to come. I'm not sure you can put together fans of either that listen to these albums all the way through without skipping a track. Both have their standout tracks, personal favorites, and forget-ables.

To close to score

Game-Changer or Pace-Keeper

All Eyez on Me was a pace-keeper. For all of the dope tracks and the handful of skip-ables, as an album, it was an evolution of the then popular Death Row vibe. I would say **Makavelli** was more of game-changer than **All Eyez on Me**.

The Score was a game-changer. It was a quantum leap

CDs, Records, & Tapes

from their first album and a precedent for their forthcoming solo albums. In some ways, it laid a template for the next few years of popular music. It was a magic-in-a-bottle moment.

2Pac - 1 point, 9 total
The Fugees - 2 points, 10 total

Rewind to February 1996 and you're at Sam Goody or the neighborhood mom & pop record store, which should you purchase first? Actually, I didn't buy either when they first dropped. I was a little disappointed in the persona that 2Pac had evolved into and I was reluctant on trying out The Fugees. Yet, eventually in '96, much like today's exercise, **The Score** was my initial purchase.

20
BATTLE OF THE POSSE CUTS: LA VS THE BAY #2
"PICTURE ME ROLLIN'" VS. "3 CARD MOLLY"

Remember when people were crossing their middle fingers and throwing up "dubs" as a gesture of West Coast love? I do. If we were to just focus on record sales, we would see the "dub" era also marks the end of the West as the dominant commercial powerhouse in Hip Hop. Sadly, the ending of that era is highlighted by the murder of Tupac. Indeed, there would be other commercially-viable and lyrically-talented MCs from the West in subsequent years, but the years spanning from **The Chronic** to **All Eyez On Me** were historical.

Only an icon like 2Pac can release multiple posthumous albums while gaining nearly mythological status. Rhyme purists' arguments about the quality of 'Pac lyrical skills consistently falls on deaf ears because whether or not you believe he was a lyrical giant, you have to acknowledge that his delivery certainly set him apart. His flow and cadence is instantly recognizable.

However, in no way was 2Pac the only giant from the West Coast. In fact before Steph, Klay, and Draymond were claiming championships, there was another team of Golden

State Warriors with championship pedigree: Xzibit, Ras Kass, and Saafir. This match-up is dedicated to West Coast and its enduring influence on Hip Hop.

These battles follow three rules:

- Must feature at least three different MCs;
- Cannot be from the same crew; and
- Will be from a similar region.

MCs are scored with a relay-race inspired point system:

- 0 – Maybe y'all should have just sang the hook;
- 1 – Okay, we hear you;
- 2 – Whoa, that was nice!; and
- 3 – DAANNGG, I gotta learn those bars!

2Pac vs. Ras Kass

Here we are: an icon vs an iconic MC. It really doesn't get better than this. I'll state my bias up front – I've listened to "Picture Me Rollin'" a couple of hundred times more than I've listened to "3 Card Molly." I even shout it out in one of my novels. But I assume that these tracks were made to evoke different responses. "Rollin'" is a melodic sh**-talkin' anthem while "Molly" is a demonstration of lyrical skill. Agree? Either way, 'Pac gets us going with:

> *Picture me rollin' in my 500 Benz*
> *I got no love for these ni***a, there's no need to be friends*
> *They got me under surveillance*
> *That's what somebody be tellin'*

> *Know there's dope bein' sold, but I ain't the one sellin'...*
> *... Mama, I'm still thuggin', the world is a war zone*
> *My homies is inmates, and most of them dead wrong*
> *Full grown, finally a man, just schemin' on ways*
> *To put some green inside the palms of my empty hands*
> *Just picture me rollin'*
> *Flossin' a Benz on rims that isn't stolen*
> *My dreams is censored, my hopes are gone*
> *I'm like a fiend that finally sees when all the dope is gone*
> *My nerves is wrecked, heart beatin'*
> *And my hands are swollen*
> *Thinkin' of the G's I'll be holdin'; picture me rollin'.*

When listening or reading those lyrics, images come to mind. Fans can "see" 'Pac's circumstances, sense his hope, and feel his frustration. It's that kind of emotion that keeps fans talking about him decades after his assassination.

Ras Kass is more than just the Waterproof MC, he is a damn lyrical colossus. Remember how dudes would claim to be your favorite rapper's favorite rapper? Yeah, I'd bet many of our favorite rappers favorite rapper is Ras. From the first track I heard of his, "Remain Anonymous," to the recently released **Soul On Ice 2**, Ras been "on a roll like toilet tissue." Here on "3 Card Molly," he spits:

> *I got three-oh-fo's in three-one-oh*
> *On section eight, with multiple one-eighty-sevens*

CDs, Records, & Tapes

> *Sport a Marilyn Manson t-shirt when I die and*
> *go to heaven*
> *Smoke a beady, scrape my lungs, smoke the resin*
> *Remember the name Ras Kass-ciano*
> *Get to clownin y'all punk bitches, cause I'm a*
> *Mac, like Ronald*
> *I make Mac make money, and mack murder*
> *wack rappers*
> *My Makaveli verse Bomb First, the Mac-11'll*
> *gat cha*
> *When I get at cha, the situation tenses*
> *Fatality (Toasty!) before you ever reach your*
> *senses*
> *Got so-called riders, crashing into brick fences*
> *Like my name was Al Fayed so you die, like that*
> *white princess*
> *If you lookin for sympathy, you better look*
> *Between R and T, in the f****** dictionary*
> *See the object of the game is to win, stack some*
> *ends, sippin Henn'*
> *Whip a Benz and leave it to your next of kin.*

When it comes to 'Pac, it's hard to be objective – nostalgia and sentiment are HUGE influences on objectivity. But Ras? Even if you just read those lines and missed out on his sarcastically cocky flow, those are some impressive bars.

2Pac -2.5 / Ras Kass – 2.5
"Picture Me Rollin'"– 2.5 / "3 Card Molly" – 2.5

Big Syke vs. Saafir

Those are some tough MCs to follow, real tough. But since "Rollin'" is a sh** talkin' anthem, Syke keeps it going with:

> *I got keys comin' from overseas*
> *Cost a ni**a 200 G's*
> *I'm a street commando, Nino for example*
> *This lavish lifestyle is hard to handle*
> *So I got to floss 'cause I'm more like a boss player*
> *Thug, branded to be a women-layer*
> *So many player haters, imitators steady swangin'*
> *Make me wanna start back bangin'...*

Alright. Next up to bat is Saafir who swings with:

> *The un-edited medic, on the cut, with a degree in metaphysics*
> *A doctor, with a lot of patients/patience*
> *And perseverance — flows like an ocean liner*
> *That sails/sales like a clearance, I'm bilingual*
> *Fly like a flamingo, I'm a pitcha, everything I freak*
> *I heat like Al Pacino, you don't like me baby*
> *You ain't happy, you need some Ecstasy*
> *Now you in my properties, but you have to pay my equity*
> *For the lowest point in my character*
> *I'll reach the highest place in the house when I rock*
> *Like the Qu'ran, fuse hot, fluid with flavor like buillion cube*
> *Been this way since I was fourteen*

And like this I been runnin s*** without the use of
    Sportscreme
Rippin up tracks like immigrant Chinese.

Lyrical? Yes. Saafir's flow on the track? Man, I don't know. It messed with my ability to appreciate his wordplay. Flow or not, it's still more outstanding than "keeeeeyyys from overssssseeeaaasss."

Big Syke -1 / Saafir- 2
"Picture Me Rollin'"– 3.5 / "3 Card Molly" – 4.5

CPO & 2Pac vs. Xzibit

Yep, a two-on-one fast break with CPO and 'Pac passing the mic to each other and Xzibit backpedaling on defense. CPO starts:

> *I gots to get the f**k up in it, formulate a caper*
> *'Cause a ni**a straight sufferin' from lack of*
>   *havin' paper*
> *My bi**h fin' to have a bastard, see?*
> *So I needs to hit a lick, drastically.*

Dude's money situation is tight and he needs to come up. 'Pac to the rescue with bars not really worth re-typing but if you ever seen two ball players pass back and forth on a fast break, then picture 'Pac in a give & go back to CPO for the layup:

> *Move smooth as a m***********, me and my nine*
> *I'm cool as a m***********, I'ma get mine*
> *Now we satisfied, got the pockets on swoll*

> *Boss Hogg and this 'Pac ni**a, picture us rollin'.*

Yet, before CPO can lay that joint off the glass, Xzibit raises up for the block:

> *Fricasseed emcee, we be the ones that keep the*
> *pu**y hot*
> *Xzibit livin life, like a bull inside a china shop*
> *Strippin everything, see you ain't even got a dime*
> *to drop*
> *Go ahead and call the cops, you ain't said nathin*
> *Jerry Spring-you out the studio, then Suge*
> *Knight you*
> *To the parkin lot, ni**as ain't ready for all this*
> *heat we got*
> *Picture yourself crushin Xzibit with your*
> *tough talk*
> *That's like Christopher Reeves doing the Crip*
> *walk.*

Game over. CPO's layup blocked all up into the bleachers. Those last four lines seal the deal.

CPO -1 / Xzibit – 2
"Picture Me Rollin'" – 4.5 / "3 Card Molly" – 6.5

Without a doubt, "Picture Me Rollin'" was the bigger hit. It was the jam – shoot, even my 13-year-old daughter knows it. But in a battle featuring lyrics? It can't hold up against the Golden State Warriors.

21

JUST ONE: SUMMER 1996
THE STAKES IS HIGH VS. REASONABLE DOUBT

The two camps in this match-up are were possibly as far apart as the Bernie Sanders and Joe Biden camps. Released seven days apart during the summer of 1996, De La Soul's **Stakes Is High** and Jay-Z's **Reasonable Doubt** are not only contrasting flavors in Hip Hop but both of these albums dropped at a time when the culture was changing. Pac and B.I.G. had been taken from us. The mindless testosterone of gangsta rap was starting to fade and Puff Daddy's shiny suit reign was still ahead of us.

Personally, I had graduated from college and was facing the damnedest time landing a job which prompted me going to graduate school while also providing the awareness that things often won't go as planned. I was in a melancholic place when I heard these albums; yet, I sensed that things were changing for the better in my life and in Hip Hop.

Our 0-2 point scoring system in a few categories will help determine which should have been purchased first:

1. *Pre-release history*
2. *Review of three songs*

3. How did it age / does it still sound fresh?
4. Game-Changer or Pace-Keeper

Pre-Release History

I'll be upfront – I was a reluctant De La fan. Always respected them; yet, didn't "get" them at first. However, my respect is rooted in their courage to switch things up and evolve. Their evolution helps me "hear" their lyrics better. I mean, **3 Feet High and Rising** was a huge break from the norm. They could have stayed comfortable in that lane and became gimmicky (an example of this is the Insane Clown Posse), but they didn't. They evolved. They are the truth.

De La Soul – 2 points

Until other rappers brought it up as a means of dissing Jay-Z, I had sort of forgotten his "Hawaiian Sophie" cameo. Although I was attending school on the East Coast and had access to what was up and coming in Hip Hop, Jay-Z wasn't on my radar. It wasn't until I was hanging with my man, Jay, in Atlanta when "Ain't No Ni***" started getting heavy airplay (along with "My Boo" by the Ghost Town DJs and "Whatz Up Whatz Up" by Playa Poncho – I said I was in Atlanta, man). But I don't think any of us knew that he would become the cultural colossus he is today.

Jay-Z – 1 point

Song Reviews

"Stakes Is High": Hold on, there is no way we can reflect on this song without saying with "Vibes ... vibrations."

CDs, Records, & Tapes

Alright, now we can proceed. **Stakes Is High** was the first De La CD I purchased and since I was new to the CD track shuffle feature, the title track is the first song I heard. And boy! It was an indictment on the times!

> *I say G's are making figures at a high regard*
> *And ni***s dying for it nowadays ain't odd*
> *Investing in fantasies and not God*
> *Welcome to reality, see times is hard*
> *People try to snatch the credit, but can't claim*
>   *the card*
> *Showing out in videos, saying they co-starred*
> *See, s*** like that will make your mama cry*
> *Better watch the way you spend it cause the*
>   *stakes is high.*

De La Soul – 2 points, 4 total

"Ain't No Ni***": Wait a minute – to go from the "Stakes Is High" to "Ain't No Ni***" captures this whole competition in a nutshell. Back to the song, because they use the same sample as EPMD's "It's My Thing", I had to give this track a listen. Plus, Foxy Brown? Man, let me tell you, I just have thing for a feisty spirited lady and Foxy is definitely that.

Yet, this was the beginning of my appreciation for Jay's witty off-liners like:

> *I've been sinnin' since you been playin' with*
>   *Barbie and Ken and*
> *You can't change a player's game in the 9th*
>   *inning ...*

Subject matter aside, if you know what you're listening to, then you can acknowledge the craft.

Jay-Z – 2 points, 3 total

"The Bizness": despite my lower scoring of Common's first album in a previous essay, Rashid is my man. He is solid, consistent, and a great compliment to Pos and Dove / Dave. He captures the essence of the album when he spit:

> *Do you wanna be a MC, or do you wanna serve?*
> *Do you wanna be dope, or do you wanna deal it?*
> *Moreover, this is really when De La got me to rewinding and checking again for what they said. Like when the song opened with these bars:*
> *I speak divine of God theories, no need to be high*
> *Always exhale the facts 'cause I don't inhale lie*
> *Play the greater man's game to bounce off my losses*
> *So I can earn the acres (uhh) the houses (yeah) the horses (huh)*
> *Of course it's much greater than your Benz or your Lex*
> *The engine to my comprehension is just too complex*

De La Soul – 2 points, 6 total

"Brooklyn's Finest": In addition to coming-of-age with Hip Hop, I also came of age with comic books. Back in the day, there used to be a series called **Marvel Team-Up** where they would do one story with two stars who hadn't shared a story together. When I first heard "Brooklyn's Finest", all I could hear was a Hip Hop Team-Up. To me and other fans who were just starting to know Jay-Z, this pound-for-pound, back-and-forth with B.I.G. really showed his promise.

Jay-Z:

> *While y'all pump Willie, I run up and stunt silly*
> *Scared, so you sent your little mans to come kill me*
> *But on the con-trilli, I packs the MAC-milli*
> *Squeezed off on him, left them paramedics breathin' soft on him*
> *"What's ya name?"*

B.I.G.:

> *Who shot ya? Mob ties like Sinatra (uh)*
> *Peruvians tried to do me in, I ain't paid them yet*
> *Tryin' to push 700s, they ain't made them yet*
> *Rolex and bracelets is frostbit; rings too*
> *Ni***s 'round the way call me Igloo, stick WHO?*

"Brooklyn's Finest" is a classic.

Jay-Z – 2 points, 5 total

"Itzsoweezee (HOT)" is aptly titled because it is HOT! Moreover, it still thumps. If it was an instrumental, it would outstanding; yet, the lyrics take it up another notch:

> *See them Cubans don't care what y'all ni***s do*
> *Colombians ain't never ran with your crew*
> *Why you acting all spicy and sheisty*

> *The only Italians you knew was icees, ni***s*
> *price me*
> *And then they re-emphasize it while also*
> *displaying their skills:*
> *Now here's the lead, y'all ni***a pray to hot rods*
> *and not God*
> *While Versace play you bitches like Yahtzee*
> *Crackin jokes like you Potsie*
> *(When's the last time you had Happy Days?)*
> *Blazin' up your herb to escape the maze, but the*
> *problem stays*
> *Think big get it big is my motto*
> *You can go and play your lotto*
> *I'll be singin' like baby won't you be mine*
> *You'll be pressin' rewind, you can never see mine*
> *Keep your eyes focused, you can't touch this or*
> *quote this*
> *Style is crazy bogus so you can't try to approach*
> *this ...*

De La Soul – 2 points, 8 total

"Can I Live": because "Itzsoweezee" was my favorite beat, I'll go with my favorite beat on Reasonable Doubt – the Isaac Hayes sample track, "Can I Live". Since I was vibin' to the beat so tough, the slow down helped me realize the Jay-Z was more than a show-off, materialistic, wanna-be-don, rapper. It's like all that was smoke & mirrors for the real genius behind the facade. This would become more and more apparent over time.

> *My crew and me commit atrocities like we got*
> *immunity*

You guessed it, manifest it
In tangible goods, platinum Rolex'd it
We don't lease, we buy the whole car, as you
should
My confederation, dead a nation
Explode on detonation, overload the mind of a
said patient
When it boils to steam, it comes to it
We all fiends, gotta do it: even righteous minds go
through this
True this, the streets school us to spend our
money foolish
Bond with jewelers and watch for intruders
I stepped it up another level, meditated like a
Buddhist.

Jay-Z – 2 points, 7 total

How Did It Age?

Despite your preference, both of these albums aged about the same. Lyrically and sonically, they both continue to resonate with their fans. For me, particularly back in '96, I was gaining an awareness of how wide Hip Hop's influence was becoming. As a soon-to-be teacher, I was acutely sensitive about our responsibility in the messages we share. While writing this, I kept getting stuck between De La's message and Jay-Z's craft.

To help me sift through the stalemate, I got on the phone with my guys, John and Mike. As we chopped it up, they brought up the notion of a greatest hits album. The idea being one greatest hits album covers the artist's whole catalog. I'm going to expand on their idea – if we have a 20 song greatest hits CD, how many tracks on the De La one would come from **Stakes is High**? How many on the Jay-Z one would come from **Reasonable Doubt**? That broke the stalemate for me. With this assessment of how the albums aged, I shifted to a perspective of almost an intra-artist comparison of their other work. That shift in perspective led me to:

> De La Soul – 1 point, 9 points
> Jay-Z – 2 point, 9 points

Game-Changer or Pace-Keeper

After **Stakes is High**, I worked my way back and listened to previous De La albums and noticed that they grew with each release. They are artists, not caricatures. Due to their steady and impressive evolution, **Stakes is High** is a pace-keeper.

I really can't pinpoint when the mafioso thing took off in Hip Hop. My favorite hometown rappers, AWOL, wore "full-length minks and beaver hats." So stylistically, the whole laid back, grown-a** man, who has his finances and his relationships with ladies under control – that persona was not new to me. However, on a national scale that spanned from chucks & khakis to Timberlands & camouflage jackets, **Reasonable Doubt** was a game-changer. Although Nas was already a known and respected MC, Jay-Z took the Brooklyn MC baton from B.I.G. and ran with toward record-breaking success. In the void of B.I.G.'s absence, Jay-Z was staking a serious claim as the King of New York.

> De La Soul – 1 point, 10 total
> Jay-Z – 2 points, 11 total

CDs, Records, & Tapes

This exercise in nostalgia prompts a bit of reflection. Back in '96, I bought De La first. I saw it as a "let-me-see-if-all-the-hype-is-for-real" purchase. I didn't buy **Reasonable Doubt** until years later because I erroneously assumed Jay-Z was one-dimensional. After calculating the categories, while I still would have purchased both, **Reasonable Doubt** should have been the first purchase.

22

BATTLE OF THE POSSE CUTS: DYNAMIC DUOS

"WE MADE IT" VS. "LIFE'S A BIT**"

Some of y'all might find it a bit sacrilegious to pit any song against Life's A Bit**, which I totally understand. It is without a doubt one of the banging-est Hip Hop tracks ever as well as a standout track on a classic album. However, we gain nothing by playing it safe, so let's go out on a limb and see how it matches up with Jay-Z and Jay Electronica.

Despite the twenty-year gap between these recordings, they share some similarities. They open with legendary MCs who never achieved the commercial success that their lyricism deserved and end with MCs who are perennial Hip Hop giants lyrically and commercially.

Why would I choose to pit these songs against each other? Easy, my daughter asked which did think was better and I was dumbfounded. To grant some perspective, "Life's A Bit**" was the first song I played for my birthday every year from 1994, the year I turned 20, until 2017, when my dad passed and I accepted the transition from being a young man into becoming a grown a** man. Nevertheless, AZ's line about "Keepin' this Schweppervescent street ghetto essence inside us" will always resonate with me.

Then there is "We Made It," a freestyle originally designed to take shots at Drake. At my stage of Hip Hop fandom, Drake is of little consequence; but Jay Electronica and Jay-Z on the same track?! That's some stop-what-you're-doing level stuff there (and the reason you MUST cop Jay Electronica's album). So let's get into it, here are the rules:

- Must feature at least three different MCs (this is the exception because of the four legends involved);
- Cannot be from the same crew; and
- Will be from a similar region.

Even though today's battle is more of a tag team than a relay, we will retain our usual relay scoring method with each MC being scored this way:

- 0 - Maybe y'all should have just sang the hook;
- 1 - Okay, we hear you;
- 2 - Whoa, that was nice!; and
- 3 - DAANNGG, I gotta learn those bars!

Jay Electronica vs. AZ

Some would consider Jay Electronica to be Hip Hop's Sasquatch or Loch Ness Monster because for years there have been reported sightings of an album, but regular fans have never seen it at Best Buy, iTunes, or Tidal (notice how the music purchasing mediums have changed). That changed recently and while it is hard to say whether it was worth the weight, it gets steady receptive play from me. Jay's lyrics are multilayered and thought-provoking.

> *The devil, the haters, the bloggers*
> *The papers, the labels, they labeled me*
> *But they can't relate to our struggle, my n***a*
> *We came up from slavery*
> *Apologies go out to all of my fans cause they*
> *   waited so patiently*
> *This one is for all of the lost and forgotten black*
> *   angels that prayed for me ...*

As scholars tend to say, "it's just so much to unpack." Yet, as potent of an opening as that is, AZ set the bar in a whole 'nuther galaxy when he opened with:

> *Visualizin' the realism of life in actuality*
> *F**k who's the baddest, a person's status depends*
> *   on salary*
> *And my mentality is money-orientated*
> *I'm destined to live the dream for all my peeps*
> *   who never made it ...*

Whoa. Countless Hip Hop Heads have gotten tongue-tied trying to repeat those bars. It's like we're awed and inspired. Those bars and Inspectah Deck's opening in "Triumph" are some of the best opening lines EVER. It's also like Jay came out bobbing and weaving before he threw the first jab. AZ came with an opening straight jab to the mouth (or to the ears – but you know what I mean). Yet, in a good way, we have to account for the compounding nostalgia that comes with listening to AZ. I'm going to try to work around that and go almost bar-for-bar in a vacuum. But out the gate, AZ was blazing.

As we return to Jay Electronica's verse, the beat drops right when he says:

A milli, a milli, n****s love me cause I'm ill
The greatest story ever told, n****s in the field
From Solomon to Sambo to Django, it's fact
I'm the Farrakhan of rap and I get it from the wheel
The son of WD, who hung around in the D
Who ran around in the three
The trap gods raised me ...

Historical, mystical, theological – those are of terms not often used describing bars, but they fit here and prove to us just how Jay earned his mythological status. (Plus a shout out for the Detroit reference!) But AZ can go there too:

'Cause yeah, we were beginners in the hood as Five Percenters
But somethin' must've got in us, 'cause all of us turned to sinners
Now some restin' in peace and some are sittin' in San Quentin
Others, such as myself, are tryin' to carry on tradition
Keepin' this Schweppervescent street ghetto essence inside us
'Cause it provides us with the proper insight to guide us
Even though we know, somehow we all gotta go
But as long as we leavin' thievin'
We'll be leavin' with some kind of dough
So, until that day we expire and turn to vapors
Me and my capers will be somewhere stackin' plenty papers
Keepin' it real, packin' steel, gettin' high

*'Cause life's a b**** and then you die!*

While we get the impression that Jay maybe a strict religious practitioner, AZ seems to have lost the faith and adopted the hustler's religion. Moreover, the elephant in the room is that he stole the spotlight from Nas with those bars – that is a big f*****ing deal! But dawg ... Jay Electronica, man. So it's like this, AZ came out with a sustained blazing fire, but Jay built up from a simmer to a blaze to a bonfire. See what I mean:

> *Face all on the Sphinx*
> *Story all in the wall of the pyramids*
> *N****s know the Black God saved me*
> *You can blow the nose off, that won't change it*
> *Obamacare won't heal all that anguish*
> *We came a long way from the bottom of the boat*
> *All praise to the Mahdi, we found our language*
> *Gold necklace, middle finger erected*
> *God tribe of Shabazz stylin' on the record*
> *Lost sons of Muhammad, we wildin' in the wreckage*
> *Asha du illah illaha is the message ...*

Wait a minute. Dude spits in Arabic within his flow and does not lose momentum. I mean, I'm old school and remember when King Sun did a little Spanish and French on a track, but Arabic? And still flow? Dawg. For real? The rest of the verse slows a bit, but this is a banging-a** verse!

Jay Electronica -2.5 / AZ – 3
We Made It – 2.5 / Life's A Bit** – 3

Jay-Z vs. Nas

This ain't "Takeover" vs. "Stillmatic," but it is a display of these iconic MCs doing their thing. Their respective catalogs are immense – loaded with classics, bangers, and a handful of forgettable tracks. We also have to consider this is early Nasty Nas (*I didn't hear "Live at the BBQ" until after I heard Illmatic) vs. established, philanthropist, married Jay-Z. That gap in age accounts for perspective but also leaves us with their flow and wordplay. Let's start with Jay:

> *Hop off the slave ship*
> *Popped off my chain and took it to Jacob, I got it*
>   *gold plated*
> *Walked in that b**** like "N***a we made it!"*
> *I own my own masters*
> *You know I ain't missin' no royalty statements*
> *I can't be rated (God, God), damn Hov stunt on*
>   *them haters!*

Still think Jay is one-dimensional, well, to quotethe final words of Stringer Bell, "Don't seem like ... I can say nothing that can change y'all mind ... get on with it moth**..."

> *Don't make me RRRRAA yah, n***a watch*
>   *your tone*
> *I come to court with black boxers on*
> *Y'all hella jealous of my melatonin*
> *I could black out at any given moment*
> *I'm god, G is the seventh letter made*
> *So when my arms and feet shackled I still*
>   *get paid*
> *All praises due*

> *I'm ready to chase the Yakub back into caves*
> *These are the last days, but do I seem fazed?*
> *Showed up to the last supper in some brand new*
>   *J's ...*

Man, you didn't know Jay had it in him, hunh? He went multi-layered and religiously symbolic with Jay Electronica. But Nas can't be overlooked - here's the whole verse:

> *I woke up early on my born day; I'm 20, it's a*
>   *blessin'*
> *The essence of adolescence leaves my body, now*
>   *I'm fresh and*
> *My physical frame is celebrated 'cause I made it*
> *One quarter through life, some godly-like thing*
>   *created*
> *Got rhymes 365 days annual, plus some*
> *Load up the mic and bust one, cuss while I*
>   *pus from*
> *My skull, 'cause it's pain in my brain vein, money*
>   *maintain*
> *Don't go against the grain, simple and plain*
> *When I was young at this I used to do my*
>   *thing hard*
> *Robbin' foreigners, take they wallets, they jewels*
>   *and rip they green cards*
> *Dipped to the projects, flashin' my quick cash*
> *And got my first piece of a**, smokin' blunts*
>   *with hash*
> *Now it's all about cash in abundance*
> *N****as I used to run with is rich or doin' years in*
>   *the hundreds*
> *I switched my motto; instead of sayin', "F**k*

CDs, Records, & Tapes

> *tomorrow!"*
> *That buck that bought a bottle could've struck the lotto*
> *Once I stood on the block, loose cracks produce stacks*
> *I cooked up and cut small pieces to get my loot back*
> *Time is illmatic, keep static like wool fabric*
> *Pack a 4-matic to crack your whole cabbage!*

Nas' storytelling is unique. It's like you can see yourself there. That is a skill significantly more complex than making words rhyme. Moreover, I was still in my hard-reluctance-to-East-Coast-Rap stage when I first heard this and became a believer with the first listen. It was Nas that made me believe the pendulum of popularity was swinging back East after years on the West.

From this exercise I've learned, it's best to stick with tracks within the same time frame. One reason is that nostalgia gets in the way of objectivity as it is clouding my ears regarding coming of age with Nas' verse.

Jay-Z – 2.5 / Nas – 2.5
We Made It– 5 / Life's A Bit** – 5.5

This match-up is like Shaquille O'Neal versus Kareem Abdul-Jabbar. "We Made It" is Shaq and "Life's A Bit**" is Kareem. If Shaq bodying Kareem in the paint, there is no-stopping Shaq. Then again, Shaq couldn't do anything against the skyhook. There is a reason Kareem is the NBA All-Time leading scorer; just like "Life's A Bit**" is an all-time Hip Hop classic that not even a great song from two legends can unseat that.

23

OUTKAST THREE-PEAT

SOUTHERNPLAYALISTICADILLACMUZIK ~ ATLIENS ~
AQUEMINI

With our last Hip-Hop Three-peat entry, we will acknowledge the brilliance of OutKast. If you are uncertain of who Big Boi and Andre 3000 are and what they stand for, allow Big Rube to explain:

> *Operating under the crooked American system*
>   *too long*
> *OutKast, pronounced outcast*
> *Adjective meaning homeless, or unaccepted in*
>   *society*
> *But let's look deeper than that*
> *Are you an OutKast?*
> *If you understand and feel the basic principles*
>   *and*
> *Fundamental truths contained within this music,*
>   *you probably are...*

Got it? Let's proceed.

With this series we are celebrating Hip Hop acts that, much like three-peat NBA champions, released three consecutive classics. Consecutive being the operative term. One of my favorite rappers, Common, has an excellent body of work; yet, he is the San Antonio Spurs of Hip Hop championships. His classics, **Resurrection** (1994), **Like Water for Chocolate** (2000), and **Be** (2005), were not back-to-back-to-back. But today's featured artist? Well, a strong case can be made for a Four-peat depending on your position on **Southernplaylisticadillacmuzik** and/or **Stankonia**. I will acknowledge that you can't lose either way; but I will keep it consistent and focus on the three-peat.

FIRST CHAMPIONSHIP – 1994 - SOUTHERNPLAYLISTICADILLACMUZIK

Where We Were

The post-Chronic era featured a preponderance of weed-smoking. Just about every other Hip Hop album had some dude coughing or making a reference to good ole Mary Jane. I'm not much a conspiracy theorist but I will say this, just a handful of years prior nearly everyone had their Africa medallions, then the cultural pride diminished and the so-high persona took center stage. I always thought that was a peculiar occurrence.

What made them outstanding

- The Dungeon Family – from the beats, to the cameos, or perhaps evening the criticism/coaching that led to the improvement of skills – it is impossible to talk about OutKast without the Dungeon Family;

- By being their authentic selves, they introduced a whole new flavor;
- Redefined the image of Southern Hip Hop. Much love to MC Shy-D and the 2 Live Crew; but, they were not regarded as MCs. Big Boi and Dre changed that.

What we could have done without

It would be too easy to harp on the interludes now, but back then? They worked and helped the flow of the album. The notion of what we could do without does not apply.

Championship Moment

"The South got something to say!" was the last line of Dre's speech at the 1995 Source Awards when they won Best New Artist. In my opinion, this is one of the best and hardest flag-planting, chest-thumping moments in Hip Hop.

How it impacted me

These were my dudes. The first rappers I identified with as peers or cool cats that are my age, going through the things I'm going through, and responding to them in ways I would respond. The fan-celebrity kinship I felt with Dre & Big Boi and the Goodie Mob, would never be replicated.

SECOND CHAMPIONSHIP – 1996 - **ATLIENS**

Where We Were

Organized Noize, the production team within the

Dungeon Family were now a known entity in music. In '95, another group from the Dungeon Family, Goodie Mob, had dropped their classic and still underrated debut album, **Soul Food**, and their success fed into the growing buzz for the new OutKast joint.

What made them outstanding

- They evolved – their presentation, lyricism, and thematic concepts took a leap forward;
- Sonic cohesion – the sequencing of ATLiens is remarkable. Each track flows into the next. It is designed/formatted as a singular experience – an album and not a bunch of singles;
- The beginning of Dre & Big Boi producing their own tracks.

What we could have done without

I'm proud to display my bias – this album is perfect.

Championship Moment

You can relive it. Go to your favorite sound system and cue up "Elevators" and within the first twelve seconds you will be transported to another worldly audio experience. They have not even started rhyming but you KNOW from the beat that this sh** is going to be on point! You also know that you sang along when they said:

> *Me and you*
> *Your momma and your cousin too*
> *Rolling down the strip on Vogues*

Coming up, slamming Cadillac doors

How it impacted me

The summer of '96 was tough times for me. I had a college degree and no job. My girlfriend tried to boost my spirits and took me on a drive through the city. We were rolling down Wyoming Avenue and listening to WJLB, when the legendary Reggie Reg announced he was going to spin the new OutKast. He plays it. The joint was so fire, he immediately plays it again. Me and my girlfriend, with mouths agape, look at each other in amazed disbelief. Oh sh**!! that joint thumped!!!

Fast forward a couple of months, I'm driving my then three and five-year-old nephews in my bench seat, two-door Ford Ranger and of course, we're listening to OutKast. Right on cue, the three-year-old turns to his brother and asks, "hey man, 'member me from school?" And the five-year-old replies, "nah, not really." Yes, I played this album so much I made an impression on the next generation.

THIRD CHAMPIONSHIP – 1998 - **AQUEMENI**

Where We Were

Hip Hop was no longer moving into the mainstream; it was becoming the mainstream. Puff Daddy's Shiny Suit Era was in full swing and Hype Williams videos were mini-movies. Cash Money records was ascending. The Neo-Soul sound was taking over R&B and Lauryn Hill was becoming a super-duper star.

What made them outstanding

- Dre's presentation definitely established his eccentrics while Big Boi was still the ATL player with whom we were accustomed. Their imagery was the balancing opposites that the album title invoked;
- A guest spot from Raekwon? A respected New York MC on a track with some MCs from the South? That was unprecedented;
- Many believe this is their best album. I really, really, really like it; but my heart remains with **ATLiens**. Nevertheless, this joint was SLAMMIN'! I mean, this was "the hardest sh** since MC Ren."

What we could have done without

In a random shuffling of the CD, "Nathaniel" may leave you scratching your head. But it flows well in a sequential listen of tracks. To this day, my man, John, uses this as his go-to freestyle when he's being silly.

Championship Moment

The Source crowning them with five mics on the original review, not the retrospective ones. Before the internet and social media were norms, **The Source** was the Hip Hop bible. The Source reviewers were hella stingy with the 5 mic rating which made the albums who were bestowed the honor, even more impressive.

How it impacted me

By now, you have figured that in my longing for

ATLiens, **Aquemini** got less play. That does not diminish its' classic status one bit; yet, it does connote that the personal bond I had with OutKast wasn't the same. They weren't just my guys. They were our guys because they soaring upward in celebrity status – an ascension they deserved. **Aquemini** and **The Miseducation of Lauryn Hill** trigger the same type of nostalgia for me as they embody growing diverse sounds and that growth and diversity matched how my life was changing. To that effect, I was still growing with OutKast.

Championship Reflection

OutKast's fourth album, **Stankoni**a, was a beast!! I took to it more than **Aquemini**. Think back when you first heard Dre spit:

> *Inslumnational, underground*
> *Thunder pounds when I stomp the ground*
>   *(WOO!)*
> *Like a million elephants and silverback*
>   *orangutans*
> *You can't stop the train...*

More impressive than that was the Organized Noize produced "So Fresh, So Clean."

Even with their steady progression in artistry, lyricism, and hits, I don't think anybody could have predicted the mega-smash that was **Speakerboxxx / The Love Below** – which I will proclaim as Hip Hop's best double album. It is certified diamond in sales which makes it the BIGGEST selling Hip Hop album ever.

How is that for "Two Dope Boyz in Cadillac"? Dre wasn't bullsh***ing when he said the South had something to say.

With a unique blend of originality, lyrical skill, the courage to evolve, and some dope beats, OutKast are without a doubt, Hip Hop Three-peat Champions! (Actually, Four-peat, but that's another essay for another day and a fact that separates them from A Tribe Called Quest).

> *Even the sun goes down, heroes eventually die*
> *Horoscopes often lie, and sometimes 'y'*
> *Nothin' is for sure, nothin' is for certain, nothin'*
>   *lasts forever*
> *But until they close the curtain, it's him and I:*
>   *Aquemini.*

24

BATTLE OF THE POSSE CUTS: SOUTHERN EDITION

"MAKE 'EM SAY UNHH!!!" VS. "DIRTY SOUTH"

This Battle of the Posse Cuts heads back to the Dirty South and in doing so, it's only right that we pay respect to Cool Breeze, the man who coined the term. I agree with those who believe he is the Dungeon Family's underrated MC. Choosing between "Dirty South" or "Watch for the Hook" was a challenge; but I am sure that "Dirty South" not only represents Cool Breeze's influence but also just how seriously the Dungeon Family had things on lock.

But if the Dungeon Family was one of the first networks of Southern rappers to really achieve national significance, then No Limit Records certainly solidified the South's permanent imprint on Hip Hop. If you thought they were just Pen & Pixel Graphics best customers, you ... man, I don't know what to tell you besides you missed something special.

This battle follows these rules:

- Must feature at least three different MCs (to balance today's battle, Silk the Shocker will sit this one out);

CDs, Records, & Tapes

- Cannot be from the same crew; and
- Will be from a similar region.

Each MC is scored with the following relay-race inspired point system:

- 0 - Maybe y'all should have just sang the hook;
- 1 - Okay, we hear you;
- 2 - Whoa, that was nice!; and
- 3 - DAANNGG, I gotta learn those bars!

Master P vs. Cool Breeze

Nope, P's opening bars do not belong in the pantheon of Hip Hop's best opening lyrics. But maannnn, the energy? "Make 'Em Say Unhhh!!!" preceded the popularity of Lil' Jon's Crunk movement; yet, Beats By The Pound's production could easily feel as crunk as the crunkest joint you ever heard. Master P leads the charge with:

> *N***a, I'm the colonel of the mothef***in' tank*
> *Y'all after big thangs, we after big bank*
> *Third Ward hustlas, soldiers in combat*
> *Convicts and dealers and killers with TRU tats*
> *Never gave a f**k bout no hoes on our riches*
> *And n****as come short, I'm diggin ditches*
> *M.P. pullin stripes, commander-in-chief*
> *And fools run up wrong,*
> *N***a I'm knockin out some teeth...*

If you were going to roll-up on P or anyone riding the No Limit tank, then the loss of your fronts was going to be the result. Speaking of rolling-up, "Dirty South" opens with the law rolling-up which sets a more somber tone than the hilarious introduction by Rappin' 4-Tay on "Make 'Em Say Unhhh!!!" But yo, when that countdown starts – "1 to da 2 da 3 da 4" ... get ready because it's about to get hella real and who better to bring the real than Cool Breeze:

> *Now if dirty Bill Clinton fronted me some weight*
> *Told me to keep two, bring him back eight*
> *And I only brought him five and stuck his a** for*
>   *three*
> *Do you think that Clampett will sick his goons*
>   *on me?*

Folks that argue about how much better Hip Hop used to be often bring up the notion that the music taught listeners something or made them think. While we know not all old school tracks made people think, with these bars Cool Breeze achieves that feat. He presents the hypocrisy and exploitation within the drug game. A perspective like that is way more insightful than braggadocio about spoils of hustlin' or how to mindlessly kill people that look like you. Master P definitely jumps the thing off but Cool Breeze throws an unexpected hook.

Master P -1 / Cool Breeze – 2
"Make 'Em Say Unhhh!!!" – 1 / "Dirty South" – 2

Fiend vs. Big Boi

If Cool Breeze is the unheralded member of the Dungeon Family then Fiend is the unheralded No Limit Soldier. As I've come to learn, being the laidback spirit among a collection of animated voices lends itself to being overlooked.

Those in the know or that have an ear or eye for such things, know better than overlooking the low-key dude. Fiend's flow and bars won't allow him to be overlooked:

> *Fiend exercisin his right of exorcism,*
> *Bustin' out the Expedition*
> *Bullets choppin haters business to about the size*
>   *of prisms our mission*
> *They heard we scary, No Limit mercenary*
> *No tellin how bad it get, because the worst'll vary*
> *I heard you make em worry, that this for the loot*
> *They intimidated by the rounds that the tank*
>   *shoot*

When taking a reflective view of the entire OutKast catalogue, it is obvious that Big Boi improved as an MC with each album. On this track, we still hear **Southernplayalistic** Big Boi, whose aspirational pimp bars do not match Fiend's intricacy:

> *Right, well if pimpin' be a sport I be bein' the wide*
>   *receiver*
> *That n***a B-I-G will make ya'll n***as believers*
> *Sippin' on Cuervo Gold off in the club drunk as*
>   *f**k*
> *Callin' them hoes "b****es" and smokin' my*
>   *weed up*

Fiend – 2 / Big Boi – 1
"Make 'Em Say Unhhh!!!" – 3 / "Dirty South" – 3

Mia X vs. Cool Breeze

Any fool who discredited female MCs must have never heard "the unladylike diva, lyrical man eater" Mia X. She brings it, every time, just like when she spits:

> *We capitalize and monopolize on everything we see keep pistols drawed*
> *And cocked, we got the industry locked, we can't be stopped, too hot*
> *Check the spots that we got, on Billboard*
> *This Tank can set up roadblocks, we fadin all you hoes*
> *Want some mo? Then let's go, stretch you out like elastic*
> *Zip that a** up in plastic, have ya folks pickin caskets*
> *We drastic, our tactics is homegrown in the ghetto*
> *So feel the wrath of this sista, it's like you fightin 10 n****s*
> *Forget the baby boys, it's the biggest mamma Mia.*

Yessir! Mia X could bring the heat! But you know who else brings it? Cool Breeze. Big shout out to blogger Christina Lee – because from her piece, I learned that Dirty South is originally Cool Breeze's song. Maybe that's why he has two verses on the track. He doesn't disappoint:

> *See never did I think when I got grown*
> *That some pee wee sacks had been done took this town*

> *See, life's a b****h, then you figure out*
> *Why you really got dropped in the Dirty South*
> *See in the 3rd grade this is what you told*
> *You was bought, you was sold*
> *Now they sayin' Juice left some heads cracked*
> *I betcha Jed Clampett want his money back*
> *See East Point Atlanta threw this road block*
> *Talkin' 'bout all this blow traffic got to stop*
> *So the big time players off John Freeman Way*
> *Had to find themselves another back street to take*
> *We didn't understand, "Naw n***a, that money*
>   *ain't yours"...*

Think about some of the Hip Hop tracks you find the most memorable. I bet a number of them include MCs who told a story. The best ones have stories that listeners can "see." In Cool Breeze's case, he provides an almost singalong flow with seemingly simple lines packed with layers of meaning and local slang. Here's what separates him from Mia X in this contest: I just enjoyed Mia's fire but as Dirty South ending beats fades, I have consistently found myself re-rapping Breeze's bars. This one is close.

Mia X – 2 / Cool Breeze – 2.5
"Make 'Em Say Unhhh!!!" – 5 / "Dirty South" – 5.5

Mystikal vs. Big Gipp

Talk about a contrast in styles – Mystikal's animated Southern preacher inflections vs. Big Gipp's effortless cool. But when we consider No Limit and factor the combination of a super hype song with an ultra energetic MC? Well, damn.

> *I'm that n***a that rappers look up to when they*
>   *won't know how to do it*
> *Used to be the little bitty skinny motherf****r*
>   *with the braids in his hair*
> *Used to live on Tchoupitoulas*
> *I done paid my dues, but still played the blues*
> *N***a play me like you was scared to lose*
> *I'm still a fool, you ain't heard the news*
> *I'm with them No Limit n***a, makin' major*
>   *moves*
> *I won't stop now, b***h, I can't stop*
> *You can't stop me, so b***h don't try we*
> *We TRU soldiers, we don't die*
> *We keep rollin, na-nah-nah-nah-nah.*

Whoa. Whew. I'm not sure if I heard Gipp ever spit like that; which he shouldn't because he has his own style. Almost like a wise OG, Gipp's seen-it-all-before persona is apparent when he goes:

> *Now that Cobras got the boys on Delowe on*
>   *they back*
> *Gipp hollered at Miss Ann, she said they didn't*
>   *get trapped*
> *Behind the black, behind green, behind the*
>   *red tint*
> *Dealers breaking off that blow up for those*
>   *woodchips*
> *A lot of faces ain't around, a lot of folks got shot*
> *Scatta Mack droppin' G's while that Cristal pop*
> *Been on the grind with Cool Breeze, droppin'*
>   *pounds with B*
> *Eric Neal is the coolest from my century.*

In this contest, that's not enough to top Mystikal.

Mystikal – 2 / Big Gipp – 1
"Make 'Em Say Unhhh!!!" – 7 / "Dirty South" – 6.5

In hindsight, "Make 'Em Say" was the bigger hit while the "Dirty South" is more of a classic. Both made huge impacts when they were released, but head to head? There's no stopping the No Limit Tank. UUNNNNHHH!!!

25
JUST ONE: SEPTEMBER 1998
MOM DEF AND TALIB KWELI ARE BLACK STAR VS. AQUEMINI

This is the hardest one yet.

I can't believe I'm writing this: Mos Def & Talib Kweli or Andre 3000 & Big Boi in a head to head? I'm about to show my age but remember when Hulk Hogan and Mr. T went up against Roddy Piper and Mr. Wonderful? That's how big of a match-up this is to me.

Back in 1998, I placed a priority on how good a CD sounded good in my car, which explains my No Limit Records purchases. However, I still valued unique and talented lyricists. A fact that makes September 1998 an important month in my Hip Hop fandom and drives this match-up. A match-up that we will score in a handful of categories to determine whether **Mos Def & Talib Kweli Are Black Star** or **Aquemeni** should have been our initial purchase. Emphasis on "initial" because any real Hip Hop fan owns both. We will score the following categories from 0-2 to help us come up with a total score:

1. *Pre-release history*
2. *Review of three songs*

3. *How did it age / does it still sound fresh?*
4. *Game-Changer or Pace-Keeper*

Wait, one more thing – I know that Mos Def goes by Yasiin Bey nowadays. However, since we are discussing an album from the past with his then-moniker as a part of the title, I'm going to refer to him as Mos Def in this essay.

Pre-Release History

In 1998, I had not heard of Black Star. I had finished grad school and moved back to Michigan which compromised my access to emerging styles in Hip Hop. Moreover, the label, Rawkus Records, was introduced as the place where "ole boy from the Hip Hop Shop" got a track on an album (Eminem on **Soundbombing II** in 1999). Perhaps I was an example of the national awareness of Rawkus which is we had not heard of them ... yet.

Black Star – 0 points

I frequently state, OutKast's **ATLiens** is one of my favorite all-time albums of any genre. Plus, they were backed by Organized Noize, which if I compiled an instrumental of my young adulthood, Rico, Sleepy, and Ray's sound would dominate it. Coming back to OutKast, I knew them well and was anxious for the album.

OutKast – 2 points

Song Reviews

"Definition": First, Mos does the intro with a bumping

beat- which certainly grabbed my attention. But when he spit:

> *Yo, from the first to the last of it, delivery is passionate*
> *The whole and not the half of it, forecast and aftermath of it*
> *Projectile that them blasted with, accurate assassin s****
> *Me and Kweli close like Bethlehem and Nazareth*
> ...

My life changed. Keep in mind how Hip Hop as a culture had moved to the West Coast and was then being dominated by the South. It had been years since I heard a NY MC (that I wasn't already familiar with) seize my attention.

Black Star – 2 points, 2 total

"Rosa Parks": This joint was funky as hell! Many of us were singing along with the hook. Although it takes a very hard listen and imaging from Andre's verse to fathom any remote connection to the real Rosa Parks, the song jumps out the gate and even the harmonica at the ends fits right in. Their sound evolved.

OutKast – 2 points, 4 total

"Respiration": Oh my Gawd! The beat, the bars, the imagery? For the type of Hip Hop fan I am, this is heaven via the speakers. Everybody (this track features Common) delivers Hip Hop Quotable bars.

> *It was these bars that made me a Talib Kweli fan:*
> *Look in the skies for God, what you see besides*
>   *the smog*
> *Is broken dreams flyin' away on the wings of the*
>   *obscene*
> *Thoughts that people put in the air*
> *Places where you could get murdered over a glare*
> *But everything is fair*
> *It's a paradox we call reality*
> *So keepin' it real will make you casualty of*
>   *abnormal normality*
> *Killers Born Naturally, like Mickey and Mallory*
> *Not knowin' the ways'll get you capped like an*
>   *NBA salary ...*

You ever hear something so dope, you look around to others like "did you just hear this sh**?!" That was me (and I was alone!) after hearing "Respiration" for the first time.

Black Star – 2 points, 4 total

"Skew It On the Bar-B": Raekwon the Chef on an OutKast joint? Whoa. Now, this is a treat. Big Boi wraps up this delight with:

> *Boy, I bust raps like D-boys bust gats, s****
> *We the type of people that don't bury the axe*
> *Or the hatchet, every time we see your link, we*
>   *snatch it*
> *Ridin' round our hood talkin' that dumb s****
> *Your cabbage is cracked, like plumber's a**, and*
>   *summer's grass*
> *I been in the game for a minute, seen some suckas*

> *like y'all passin'*
> *Thinkin' you're light skinned, aight then*
> *Lil' boy why you frightened?*

Can't say we saw this coming.

OutKast – 2 points, 6 total

"Thieves in the Night": I had the great fortune of teaching a Hip Hop course at my alma mater for eight years. Every single semester, I opened the class with an analysis and deep dive into "Thieves in the Night." If I was an MC, this is the track I dream I would make. I have a lot of favorites but this joint right here? It should be preserved and studied as an embodiment of true Hip Hop.

> *Speaking loudly, saying nothing, you confusing me, you losing me*
> *Your game is twisted, want me enlisted in your usury*
> *Foolishly, most men join the ranks cluelessly*
> *Buffoonish–ly accept the deception, believe the perception*
> *Reflection rarely seen across the surface of the looking glass*
> *Walking the street, wondering who they be looking past*
> *Looking gassed with them imported designer shades on*
> *Stars shine bright, but the light rarely stays on*
> *Same song, just remixed, different arrangement*
> *Put you on a yacht, but they won't call it a slave ship*

> *Strangeness, you don't control this, you barely*
>   *hold this*
> *Screaming "brand new", when they just sanitized*
>   *the old sh***
> *Suppose it's, just another clever Jedi mind trick*
> *That they been running across stars through all*
>   *the time with*
> *I find it's distressing, there's never no in-between*
> *(We either ni***s or Kings, we either bi****s or*
>   *Queens)*
> *The deadly ritual seems immersed in the perverse*
> *Full of short attention spans, short tempers, and*
>   *(short skirts)*
> *Long barrel automatics released in (short bursts)*
> *The length of black life is treated with (short*
>   *worth)* ...

Look, I had to pull the car over to the side of the road to process all that. Then I played again.

Black Star – 2 points, 6 total

"Liberation": My favorite track on the album and one of my favorite OutKast tracks ever! Guest spots by Cee-Lo and Erykah Badu and a whole funky choral-like vibe. Plus, a verse from Big Rube!! Man, this track is SLAMMING! I'll put it like this, if you never heard the song and I told you Big Boi kind of sang-rhymed this:

> *I say, to have a choice to be who you wants to be*
> *It's left up-a to me and my momma n'em told me*

You would be like, "eh." But to hear it? My friend, it is an otherworldly musical experience. They did the da** thing on this track!

One more takeaway – for all the so-called weirdness of Andre, the parallels between his artistic evolution and Cee-Lo's have more in common than is often acknowledged. I'm a fan of both and their evolution – so it is a win-win for me.

OutKast – 2 points, 8 total

How Did It Age?

Ah ha!! This is where it gets real. My youngest daughter likes to experience Hip Hop with me. When I told her I was doing this match-up, she was "Ooooooo." Then she flipped it and was like here's how you know which aged the best. She went to the playlist I keep on my phone and there it was: two **Aquemini** tracks and seven **Black Star** tracks. I guess when we get down to it, that says which aged best for me.

Black Star – 2 points, 8 total
OutKast – 1 point, 9 total

Game-Changer or Pace-Keeper

For those of us who never sat-in at the Lyricist Lounge and was otherwise removed from the burgeoning NYC ciphers, **Mos Def & Talib Kweli are Black Star** is a game-changer because we had never heard anything like this before. Come to think of it, it is probably a game-changer for those who were familiar with them.

Looking back at the time, we were just months away from "Cash Money taking over for the '99 and 2000" and

Puff Daddy was at his shiny suit pinnacle. Hip Hop was changing. But for me, I was longing for a time when as KRS-One said "a dope MC (was) a dope MC." Yasiin and Talib were saviors to me.

Aquemini was an evolutionary pace-keeper. OutKast had established themselves the dominant group from the South. They were innovative. They were funky. They had the hits and they could spit! Yes, the South (OutKast) definitely had "something to say."

> Black Star – 2 points, 10 total
> OutKast – 1 point, 10 total

A tie.

With this match-up, one group was impeded by their pre-release history. However, the fact is I hadn't heard of them (at that time) and I can't change that.

But what I would change is how long it took me to get on board with Black Star. You see, it wasn't until Mos Def, Black Thought, and Pharoahe Monch were on the cover of **The Source** that I heard of them. The article piqued my curiosity and I bought **Black on Both Sides**. I couldn't believe that dude had escaped my awareness. That album had me all the way open. Because it was so dope, it led me to purchase **Mos Def & Talib Kweli are Black Star**. I copped it during a road trip and it didn't come out of my CD player for a month.

Considering this tie and retroactively thinking about which I would have purchased first, I would make this one change. I would have bought them both on the day they dropped with one unique wrinkle, I would have purchased Black Star instead Tribe's **The Love Movement**. Looking back (and I know this sounds odd), OutKast was where I had been but Black Star was where I was headed.

26

JUST ONE: NOVEMBER 2002
QUALITY VS. PHRENOLOGY

It's easy to be nostalgic about the music of my youth, but by the time I was grown, married, and paying a mortgage – my musical purchases came with a lot more discernment. Particularly in 2002, I was not using Napster or other online mediums to explore new artists. When I spent my money, it had to be a sure thing. Few things were surer than the dilemma faced by Hip Hop Heads in November 2002 when we had to choose between Talib Kweli's **Quality** and The Roots' **Phrenology**. By this time, my money situation was better than it was when I was choosing between Big Daddy Kane and EPMD. I could afford to buy more than one; however, I preferred one at a time for a focused listen.

By now, you know the purchasing choice is broken down into the following categories and scored between 0 – 2:

1. *Pre-release history*
2. *Review of three songs*
3. *How did it age / does it still sound fresh?*
4. *Game-Changer or Pace-Keeper*

Pre-Release History

Most of us knew Talib Kweli as the other half of Black Star with Mos Def (Yasiin Bey). With Black Star, I found myself favoring Mos more but still maintaining a healthy respect for Talib. Especially, when he said:

> *Looking in the sky for God,*
> *but all I see is miles of smog,*
> *and broken dreams,*
> *finding their way,*
> *on the wings of the obscene,*
> *thoughts that people put in the air ...*

Yeah, dude could bring it. Plus, Rawkus Records was lightning in a bottle for Hip Hop aficionados.

Talib Kweli – 2 points

The Roots weren't on the come up in 2002, they were bonafide stars. They were Grammy award winners and had released four albums to wider and wider acclaim (although I still haven't heard their first album, Organix – shame on me). They had the respect of the underground and the popularity to go with it – all of which was deserved. Looking back, they had something to prove with **Phrenology**.

The Roots – 2 points

Song Reviews

"Get By" may be Talib's signature song. Produced by an

up-and-coming Kanye West, it was a banger! Talib opened with these lines:

> *We sell crack to our own out the back of our homes,*
> *we smell the musk of the dusk in the crack of the dawn,*
> *we go through episodes too, like Attack of the Clones,*
> *work 'til we break our back and you hear the crack of the bone.*

Wait, what? Yessir, he got all those syllables in cadence. I played this song so much my wife knew it by heart.

Talib Kweli – 2 points, 4 total

"Break You Off": I heard that originally this song was supposed to feature D'Angelo but to me, Musiq was a great compliment to a smoothed out Black Thought. The only way you're not feeling this song is if you're the boyfriend of the lady who got broke off.

> *You tellin' me you deeply appreciate the company*
> *The time we spend 'I feel the same*
> *It's a shame you ain't my girlfriend'*
> *Cause listen: you need a brother with that physical fix*
> *That come through in a mix for you with no head tricks or fraud*
> *You need a new position,*
> *Somethin' to get you open like its Eucalyptus got you ready to go for your's*

Come on and work wit' me,
you won't get hurt wit' me
Just keep it real and you'll get broken off certainly
Dealing with this you won't be takin' a loss;
You need to leave I'm alone and roll with the one
whose breakin' you off.

C'mon man, at some point in your life, you imagined being smooth enough to pull off a heist like that.

The Roots – 2 points, 4 total

"Shock Body" is an example of why album sequencing is so important. It wasn't released as a single but it is mandatory that I hear it immediately after "Get By." As an adult, I could better "hear" what was meant by the classification of a 'battle MC' and "Shock Body" sounds like Talib at his battle best:

Watch how Talib Kweli Greene do it
What I bring to it
You hear the theme music
My rhymes' are life support, dog, breathe to it
Rhymes are bright, the sunshine beams to it
Stop haters in their tracks like high beams
Watch the movement you was at the crime scene
screaming "I ain't do it"
But, I seen through it, it's obscene how I spew it
Martin Luther King had a dream to it, people
cling to it
I seen your momma lean to it in a green Buick
Wack ni***s get passed over so much they seem
Jewish

> *Better leave and do it now or seem foolish*
> *This music I bleed to it, I raise my seeds to it*
> *I MC with the truest in the game*
> *I stay hungry like I'm the newest in the game*
> *And stay hot like I'm bluish with the flame*
> *You heard the truth when it came*
> *And you knew it was the name that you couldn't*
>   *pronounce*
> *Now I'm all up in your mouth*

YESSIR! Talib would win the cipher with bars like that!

Talib Kweli – 2 points, 6 total

"Sacrifice" – again, a track not released as a single but one of my all-time favorites. Even now, nearly 20 years later, my daughters can recite this song as I have played it so much. ONLY Black Thought can come off like this:

> *Listen, I got you phobic off of this like arachnids*
> *Drastic, it ain't plastic it's Pro-Blackness*
> *Grown man tactics, no pediatrics*
> *The kind of track that make the comeback*
>   *miraculous*

Black Thought is more of the Truth than Paul Pierce.

The Roots – 2 points, 6 total

"Where Do We Go" is a JDilla track that sort of mellows the pace and allows listeners to grasp the ideas behind Kweli's rhymes. If there was just one bar from Kweli that I could say encapsulates the depth behind his rhymes, it is:

*What you gonna do when you gotta face
The manifestation of the words that you put in
    space ...*

Although it is a limiting label and he is much more, Kweli personifies what it means to be a conscious rapper or a thinking man's MC.

Talib Kweli – 2 points, 8 total

"The Seed 2.0": I really appreciate how The Roots sort of remix a song by another artist, maintain the integrity of the original, and introduce the original artist to a whole new audience. I bought Cody Chestnutt's album after this. Moreover, the versatility that has come to define the group is on full display on what initially comes off as a rock & roll track. But this is The Roots and you know they flipped it.

The Roots- 2 points, 8 total

How Did It Age?

These albums are essential to the soundtrack of my young manhood. So to me, they haven't aged as I still play songs from them consistently.

Note that I said "songs" and not the whole albums. Perhaps this is my Achille's Heel as a fan of The Roots, because they are so talented and diverse, their albums display those attributes. I tend to gravitate to a third of the songs on every album and replay them constantly. For another artist or group, I may be more critical of this diversity and perhaps incorrectly call it a lack of focus. Not with The Roots, because they are more than a rap group.

Which brings me back to Talib. In the way I tend to cling to about a third of the songs on every Root's album, I do the same with Talib. In his case, it's usually my preference of the beats. **Quality** is maybe the best balance of beats and lyrics in Kweli's catalog.

> Talib Kweli – 2 points, 10 points
> The Roots – 2 points, 10 points

Game-Changer or Pace-Keeper

Whoa. By a very slim margin, I'd say **Quality** was more of a game-changer because it is a solo album where we previously experienced Kweli with either Mos Def or Hi-Tek. He spit the same fire but he was the focus of the album.

The Roots maintained their quality output from their Grammy win. Additionally, both Black Thought and Kweli are featured guests on the other's album. Yet, as fans we had expectations and The Roots delivered. With Kweli, we had questions and he delivered. I REALLY feel like I'm splitting hairs right here, but....

> Talib Kweli – 2 points, 12 total
> The Roots – 1 point, 11 total

Looking back to 2002, the albums were released a week apart. My then-pregnant wife left work at lunch to amble through Best Buy and purchase **Quality** for me so that I could have it on day one. Two Fridays later, I swung by Puffer Red's to cop **Phrenology**. Both would become my favorite albums by these artists.

27

BATTLE OF THE POSSE CUTS: ALL-STAR EDITION

"SWAGGA LIKE US" VS. "MY FAVORITE MUTINY"

To quote Jay-Z, OH BABY!!!! This installment of the Battle of the Posse Cuts is an All-Star match-up that features MCs from different regions on the same track. Since there are more MCs on "Swagga ...", Lil' Wayne will sit this out as he is the man for another generation.

These battles are subjective and follow three rules:

- Must feature at least three different MCs;
- Cannot be from the same crew; and
- Will be from a similar region (this match-up's region is the Hip Hop nation).

Also note, each MC is scored this way:

- 0 - Maybe y'all should have just sang the hook;
- 1 - Okay, we hear you;
- 2 - Whoa, that was nice!; and
- 3 - DAANNGG, I gotta learn those bars!

Kanye West vs. Black Thought

In 2008, the teddy bear mascot Kanye era was over. Shortly after "Swagga Like Us," Kanye dropped **808s and Heartbreak** and I got off the Kanye train. Dude's creative chops are extraordinary and he evolved in ways artists should be free to grow; yet, there is no shade or exaggeration in saying Kanye is on some other sh**. On this track, we still hear the pesky little brother trying to show he belongs:

> *Mr. West is in the buildin'*
> *Swagger on a hundred thousand trillion*
> *Ayo I know I got it first*
> *I'm Christopher Columbus, y'all just the Pilgrims*
> *Thanksgiving, do we even got a question?*
> *Hermès, Pastelle, I pass the dressin'...*

That Christopher Columbus line feels hella awkward considering the context of some of Kanye's recent outbursts. But nevertheless, Kanye came out swinging but in this match-up, he is swinging at Black Thought. Dawg ... Black Thought. This ain't no rooty-poot, nah dawg, Black Mutha-F-ing Thought. Here's a sampling as to why he is so esteemed:

> *The long walk will burn your bare heels*
> *So throw on your boots*
> *The game camouflaged like army suits*
> *But I can see it more clear cause I came with the*
>   *Coup in here*
> *Ring the alarm and form the troops*
> *Send 'em out into the world, go to war on a fluke*
> *Eye to eye with the enemy you sworn to shoot*

> *Now I'm comin' at ya neck, sick of hearing*
> *   something wrong with me*
> *Motherf****er something's wrong with you*
> *With a Chief just way too smart to question*
> *The enemy the brothers of a dark complexion*
> *The governments of the world is shark infested*
> *They heavy on weaponry like Charlton Heston*

Kanye West – 2 / Black Thought – 3
"Swagga Like Us" – 2 / "My Favorite Mutiny" – 3

Jay-Z vs. Boots Riley

We all know Jay-Z, the god MC who is "far from being god but he works godd*** hard." He is a legend, an icon, and most certainly that dude. No MC gets to be all that without skills and this how Jay flexes his on this track:

> *(No one on the corner...) Got a bop like this*
> *Can't wear skinny jeans, 'cause my knots don't fit*
> *No one on the corner got a pocket like this*
> *So I rock Roc jeans, 'cause my knots so thick*
> *You can learn how to dress just by checkin' my*
> *   fresh*
> *Checkin' checkin' my fresh, checkin' checkin' my*
> *   fresh*
> *Follow my steps is the road to success*
> *Where the n****s know you're thorough when the*
> *   girls say yes*

Well ... those bars weren't godly. But only Jay could deliver them convincingly.

If you haven't heard of Boots Riley, man, you are missing

out. He is a part of The Coup, a hella dope group from Oakland. Look, I'll put it to you like this – he has a track called, "Me and Jesus the Pimp in a '79 Granada Last Night, "and that joint is dope. Any cat rolling with Jesus ain't scared of a god MC. Boots makes that known when he says:

> *Death to the pigs is my basic statement*
> *I spit street stories 'til I taste the pavement*
> *Tryin' to stay out the pen while we face*
>   *enslavement*
> *Had a foolproof hustle 'til they traced the*
>   *payments*
> *I was grippin' my palm around some sh***y rum*
> *Tryin' to find psalm number 151*
> *To forget what I'm owed, as I clutch the commode*
> *And read 'put down the bottle and come get*
>   *the gun'*
> *Let's get off the chain like Kunta Kinte with a*
>   *MAC-10*
> *They want us gone like a dollar in a crack den*
> *Steadily subtracting seeds & stems*
> *Mind cloudy through the wheeze and phlegm*
> *Numbing my brain off of that and the Jesus*
>   *hymns*
> *If we waiting for the time to fight, these is thems*
>   ...

"These is thems?" Yep, these are the times for which we have been preparing. In fact, we are going to break from the norm and allow Boots to finish his verse:

> *Tellin' us to relax while they ease it in. We gettin*
>   *greased again*

The truth I write is so cold, It'll freeze my pen
I'm Boots Riley it's a pleasure to meet you
Never let they punk a** ever defeat you
They got us on the corner wearing pleather and
 see thru
All y'all's gold mines they wanna deplete you
I ain't just finna to rap on the track, I'm finna to
 clap on 'em back
And it's been stackin' to that
Five hundred years before Iceberg ever leaned
 back in the 'lac
Before they told Rosa black in the back
Before the CIA told Ricky Ross to put crack in
 the sack
And Gil-Scott tradin' rappin for smack
This beat alone should get platinum plaques
I'd rather see a million of us ecstatic to scrap
Cause if we bappin' 'em back we automatically
 stacked.

Really, that verse would be a better match-up for Jay-Z's verse on the Dead Prez's "Hell Yeah" remix. But things being as they are, on this match-up, it goes like:

Jay-Z – 1 / Boots Riley – 3
"Swagga Like Us" – 3 / "My Favorite Mutiny" – 6

T.I. vs. Talib Kweli

T.I. defies the old and erroneous stereotype that Southern rappers can't spit. Not only can he spit, T.I. made hits. Prior to the release of "Swagga Like Us," I would say T.I. was the least nationally known of the MCs on the track. But he is the

MC that saves the song from mediocrity, when he came with:

> *All my verses picture-perfect all is meant to serve*
>   *a purpose,*
> *You ain't living what you kicking then you*
>   *worthless,*
> *Looking from the surface it may seem that I got*
>   *reason to be nervous*
> *Then observe my work and see that my adversity*
>   *was worth it,*
> *Verses autobiographical, absolutely classical,*
> *Last thing I'm worried 'bout is what another*
>   *rapper do,*
> *Ain't nobody hot as me*
> *Even if they rap they a** off*
> *Blast off and have outstanding qualities,*
> *Sell a lot of records I respect and salute that,*
> *But spitting real life on hot beats I'm the truth at*
> *You kick it like me no exaggeration necessary,*
> *Living revolutionary, nothing less than*
>   *legendary,*
> *Gangsta s*** hereditary, got it from my dad*
> *Flow colder than February with extraordinary*
>   *swag*

Yep, the Rubberband Man spit that swagga. Now what about Talib Kweli? Well, I'll be forthright and say I have purchased (not downloaded for free, but actually supported the artist) more Talib joints than T.I. My list of Talib favorites is long and that gives me an acute listening ear for his verse.

But the beast got it twisted, I'll untangle it
Black mind intertwined like the ropes they used to
    hang us with
This is my favorite s***, I came in the game with
    a new way to spit
That got you questioning who you bangin' with
Take it back to Imhotep
Go a step deeper like a Poor Righteous Teacher
    with Holy Intellect
Killer flow for all my real n***** left
But inform the family of the jigaboo that there's
    been a death ...

If you're new to Talib – where the hell you been? – allow me to state this fact: those are not classic Talib bars. If he was some random MC, they would be tight. But compared to Talib's body of work, the other MCs on the track, and even – in this case – T.I. In a contest where the god MC only scored a point, I can't play favorites.

T.I. – 2 / Talib Kweli – 1
"Swagga Like Us" – 5 / "My Favorite Mutiny" – 7

"Swagga Like Us" turned out to be 2004 Lakers – all that talent (and a banging beat) with just a so-so outcome. T.I. did his best Kobe Bryant but it wasn't enough. As far as "My Favorite Mutiny," despite the rare circumstance of Talib not knocking out the park, the classic verses by Black Thought and Boots Riley was like Jordan and Pippen leading the team to the win.

28

COMMON & STEVIE WONDER
PART FOUR

I imagine that there is a magical threshold for recording artist to reach. Some would say that threshold is a certain number of released albums. Some would say that a certain number of years recording or touring. Some would say that the popularity of one or a number of the artists' songs would push them to that threshold. While it would be hard to agree on the tangible dimensions of such a threshold, I believe we can agree that there is a point when an artist is widely known and / or accepted for their art.

Stevie Wonder has long passed that threshold.

Common, when factoring the relative youth of Hip Hop culture, has also reached that threshold.

I believe an attribute of having done so is when committed fans purchase the music despite what critics say. I believe another attribute is when fans who probably were not born when the artist first began, get exposed to the music and begin swearing by it with the fervor of a born-again Christian. I think one more attribute is when the artists' become known by more than their original artistic contributions. With those attributes in mind, then I propose that Common is near a threshold that Stevie Wonder crossed in the mid 70s.

At first, we covered Common's first three albums as well as three albums from the early phase of Stevie Wonder's classic period. Then we covered two of their most critically acclaimed albums and later we covered two albums that could be considered post-pinnacle productions. Which brings us to the conclusion and a look at two of their latter or most recent albums.

The Dreamer / The Believer & Jungle Fever

With these albums, even the novice listener can hear facets from both artist that are indicative of their genius. Yet, I would wager that of those who purchased these albums, more than half of those purchases were driven by name recognition or a vote of confidence developed from earlier works. In this case, Stevie has some advantages with the most notable being his extensive body of remarkable work. Another advantage is the **Jungle Fever** album was a soundtrack for a popular movie of the same name. When I was a child, my father told me that songs take on a greater meaning when there is a memory attached to them. I remember **Jungle Fever** as a powerful movie. This very good album by Stevie Wonder is bolstered by the success of Spike Lee's movie. Perhaps it is the ingenuity of cross-marketing or something else. Whatever it was, it is safe to say the soundtrack helped the movie and the movie helped the soundtrack.

I may be the only fan or perhaps one of a handful who upon seeing the cover of **The Dreamer / The Believer** thought of the effects of the *"Can You Feel It?"* music video by the The Jacksons. Nevertheless, as usual, Common brings it lyrically. My favorite track on the album was "Gold" (seriously, you should listen to this joint while reading the lyrics - Common does his thing). "Gold" has evolved into one of my all-time favorite Common tracks if only for the fact that it embodies the notion of looking-back-on-where-I've-been. Liking "Gold" so much compromised my listening experience with the rest of the album. To extend the **Jungle Fever** parallels, "Gold "was as memorable as "These Three Words." I can take that parallel a step further and say "Ghetto Dreams" was as memorable as "Jungle Fever" (the song). I'm convinced that snapshots from the "Ghetto Dreams" video are taken from some of the decayed areas of my hometown. Those dispiriting snapshots are offset by the beautiful sister in the video, plus the guest verse from Nas.

Nobody's Smiling & Conversation Peace

Both of these albums brought about my worst attribute as a music fan - being so enraptured with one song that I seldom listen to rest of the album. The first time I was diagnosed with this affliction was with Goapele's **Even Closer** when "Closer" became one of my all-time favorite songs (of any genre). The next time it flared-up was with The Roots' **The Tipping Point** and the opening song, "Star / Pointro." In those instances as with **Nobody's Smiling** and **Conversation Peace**, I have heard all of the songs on the album at least once. Yet, both albums contains one standout track that encapsulates my fondest memories of the album.

"For Your Love" exemplifies some of the components that makes Stevie's music magical. Is the song romantic or inspirational? Do you use it to convey to your innermost sentiments to your significant other? Or do you use it during moments of reflective introspection? "For Your Love" can cover those emotions and possibly others. The transcendence of Stevie's music is what makes him so legendary. His songs cannot be limited to one category or mood.

As a consumer who prefers to purchase cds and then upload my favorite tracks onto my iPod, the **Nobody's Smiling** cd is still in my car awaiting the road trip when I listen with focused attention to it in its' entirety. I look forward to giving this cd its full due. In doing so, I aim to avoid my dreaded "only-hearing-my-favorite-track" ailment. The opening track, "The Neighborhood," makes it very hard to counter that ailment. The opening bars sung by James Fauntleroy, while not quite as potent, reminded me of Cee-Lo's Free on Goode Mob's **Soul Food** and that's a fantastic way to start an album! Then No I.D. (the producer) mixes in Curtis Mayfield's "Other Side of Town" and I was totally blown. "Other Side of Town" is one song on Mayfield's amazing **Curtis** album, an album that I can sing along and play "air instruments" with on every song. I often refer to my father's influence on my musical tastes, but my love for Curtis comes directly from my mother. My mom is pretty reserved but when "Move On Up" plays, she gets to shimmying her shoulders and grinning from ear-to-ear. All of those sentiments surfaced when I heard No I.D.'s sample choice and the good times didn't stop there!

As he consistently does, Common brings it lyrically. Sometime ago, my good friend, Kofi, made a distinction between a "hungry" Common and regular Common. As I understood Kofi, "The B**** In You" is an example of the hungry Common and "Blue Sky" is an example of regular Common. I can't say with 100% accuracy if those were Kofi's sentiments but the distinction stuck with me. I should also add that making distinctions with Common's music is akin to saying you prefer Cadillac CTS-V over the CTS - either way, with a Cadillac, you're winning. Yet to the point about "hungry" Common, on "The Neighborhood," we hear the full throttle of Common's CTS-V engine. Also on "The Neighborhood," we (by that I'm assuming older Hip Hop fans) are introduced to Lil' Herb. I spent sometime hanging with a twenty year-old who attends college in Chicago and he had a whole collection of Lil' Herb songs. It was hard for me to follow all the songs but that maybe has more to do with my age than to do with Herb's skills. In addition to digging Herb's bars, I also liked Vince Staples lines in "Kingdom."

One thing that I hope Hip Hop culture can avoid is the clash between generations. By that I mean, imagine the potency of promise that could have been had there been more synergy between the Civil Rights Movement and the Black Power Movement. Instead of being fractioned into the old vs. the young, both movements could have benefitted tremendously from the other. In contemporary Hip Hop culture, there is a tendency for some of the older fans to talk down on the music created by younger artists. Truth be told, the music of younger artist reflects their reality. Some of the younger artists are talented and some are making mindless music; the same of which could be said of Hip Hop artists and rappers of my generation. By introducing Lil' Herb and Vince Staples to the older generation, I believe Common is acting as a generational ambassador. Common is an established artist and uses his platform for some younger cats to "get-on." I have tremendous respect for that.

So here we are, we have taken a look at Common's music via the lens of Stevie Wonder's albums. We have charted Common's evolution from his first album which shortly followed his feature in the Unsigned Hype section of **The**

CDs, Records, & Tapes

Source magazine to his one of his latest albums where in addition to making wonderful music, he bridges generations within our culture. While I like some Common albums more than others, the truth is that an analysis such as these prove that Common is an important contributor to Hip Hop culture. Which makes it possible to describe him in these three words: **Common is Classic.**

29

JUST ONE: LATE SUMMER 2005
LATE REGISTRATION VS. THE MINSTREL SHOW

If you're a fan of **The Wire**, remember how Omar would tense his face, shake his head, and sinisterly state, "indeed"? That's how I feel going into this match-up. I'm going to get real technical on the criteria – in previous essays, we matched albums that were released in the same month. These albums were released in different months but within two weeks of each other – so we're going with that.

By late summer 2005, I was not experimenting with my music purchases anymore. If I copped a new cd it was because I was already a fan or the buzz was so strong I had to check it out for myself. I bought, enjoyed, and still play both of these albums.

To determine which we should have purchased first, we will assign 0-2 points in the following categories:

1. *Pre-release history*
2. *Review of three songs*
3. *How did it age / does it still sound fresh?*
4. *Game-Changer or Pace-Keeper*

CDs, Records, & Tapes

Pre-Release History

I'm one of those who believe **The College Dropout** was Kanye's best album. Dude has had a truckload of hits and has certainly found rather unique ways to stay relevant, but back in '05? The anticipation of him keeping up with or topping **The College Dropout** was high.

Kanye West – 2 points

The bonafide backpackers of Hip Hop would shame you if you had not heard Little Brother's first album, **The Listening**. I had not. But thanks to Okayplayer, I learned about their **Chitlin' Circuit EP** but I still didn't cop it. However, the perfect score from Rap Reviews for **The Minstrel Show** was enough to push me into action – I was not disappointed.

Little Brother – 1 point

Song Reviews

"Gold Digger" was a HUGE hit and eventually a self-fulfilling prophecy. Add on the momentum Jamie Foxx had from his award-winning depiction of Ray Charles and you're talking about a monster smash! It was now a fact, Kanye was even bigger than he was before.

Kanye West – 2 points, 4 total

"Lovin' It" is arguably the best track on the album. First of all, I am a HUGE fan of The Stylistics so the sample and introduction had me hooked from the jump. 9th Wonder has a bangin' body of work, but if I could only have one beat from him – it would be this one. Pooh and Phonte display their usually good synergy and Joe Scudda is icing on the cake. This song is a must-have in your current rotation.

Little Brother – 2 points, 3 total

"Diamonds from Sierra Leonne (remix)": On his next album, Kanye acknowledges that his "big brother came through and kicked my a**." The said big brother is Jay Z and here and in subsequent tracks together Jay is clearly the Magic Johnson to Kanye's James Worthy. I'm getting off-topic here BUT that's why the new Jay Electronica is so dope – it features an MC who is not outshined by Jay Z, they flow together as well as Raekwon and Ghostface.

Kanye West – 2 points, 6 total

"Not Enough": Looking back, some would say this song is an indicator for the direction Phonte would go towards with The Foreign Exchange's **Connected** album. No argument on that. It should be noted that **The Minstrel Show** is a marvelously sequenced album! Every song and every skit flows seamlessly. It is an enjoyable comprehensive listen. With that said, if "Not Enough" randomly came on your shuffle, you'd bob your head to it.

Little Brother – 2 points, 5 total

"Touch the Sky" jumps out with a slamming Curtis Mayfield sample and its all good from there. This was my first time hearing Lupe and I became a fan. Moreover, as I progress through life and experience my share of disappointments, I recall Kanye's line:

> *Dog, I was havin' nervous breakdowns*
> *Like "Man, these ni***s that much better*
>   *than me?*

But guess who blew up or touched the sky? Yep, Mr. West.

Kanye West – 2 points, 8 total

"Slow It Down" is another track that fits seamlessly into the album's overall groove while managing to pique the listener's ear with some real-a** young man talk.

> *Sometimes I think I'm from another world*
> *When I'm trynna tell a woman just exactly*
>   *where I stand that*
> *I want a girl, when I want a girl*
> *And when I don't want a girl*
> *I want a girl who understands that*

Although Phonte can punch you in the face with a one-line zinger, he consistently grabs listeners with relatability over a few lines that prompt a bit of introspection.

Little Brother – 2 points, 7 total

How Did It Age?

It is no doubt that the production, marketing, and overall energy behind **Late Registration** was significantly bigger. Kanye really was doing his thing and I believe it was with this album where he cemented his fame.

Little Brother was at best, under-marketed, and probably more truthfully, ignored by their record company. What should have been their national showcase – in terms of promotion – ended up being overlooked and forgotten. Perhaps that is the reason they soon left the record company. BUT do not let record company shenanigans make you sleep on **The Minstrel Show**, it bumps!

I'm going to use two different albums to illustrate my perspective with these albums. **The Miseducation of Lauryn Hill** is a classic and it also compromised of different types of songs that prompt different listening moods. OutKast's **ATLiens** is a classic album that you can listen to, straight through, one mood. In this match-up, **Late Registration** would be more like **The Miseducation ...** while **The Minstrel Show** would be ATLiens.

> Kanye West – 2 points, 10 points
> Little Brother – 2 points, 9 points

Game-Changer or Pace-Keeper

This is where we get nit-picky. Late Registration is a pace-keeper. It builds on the vibe of **The College Dropout** and bridges to **Graduation**. There is a reason for the recurring Teddy Bear Mascot. However, even in keeping pace, Kanye improved.

Is **The Minstrel Show** a game-changer? In one way, it is the end of something special as the group shrank from a trio to a duo. For some, like me, it was the "big" release of some underground MCs – eh, maybe I'm reaching. It was a game-changer for me because it was my introduction to the group.

It is a pace-keeper to long time fans because the promise they experienced on **The Listening** shined brighter on this album.

Kanye West – 1 point, 11 total
Little Brother – 2 points, 11 total

A tie.

Really, different fans would choose the one that fits their preference but would not at all be disappointed by the other. I contemplated the Skip-A-Track test but Kanye has so many tracks, that should you skip a handful, you still have nearly an hour of quality music. It's hard to write this a not revisit the disappointment of Little Brother getting shafted by their record company. But had that not happened would we have gotten The Foreign Exchange? Pooh's albums? Phonte's albums? I don't know. I do know Phonte is one of my top five MCs and he out rhymes Kanye on Kanye's wittiest days. But between these albums? It's six in one hand, half-of-a-dozen in the other – you can't lose.

30

BATTLE OF THE POSSE CUTS: SOUTHERN LEGENDS

"STAY FLY" VS. "INTERNATIONAL PLAYER'S ANTHEM"

This Battle of the Posse Cuts shows how a grown man still longs for the music of his youth. I suppose years after their primes, these artist dropped these hits and they were slammin'! Before we dive into them, note that our match-ups will be coordinated so that every MC is scored. This battle follow three rules:

- Must feature at least three different MCs;
- Cannot be from the same crew (despite both songs being connected to the Three 6 Mafia); and
- Will be from a similar region.

The scoring is:

- 0 - Maybe y'all should have just sang the hook;
- 1 - Okay, we hear you;
- 2 - Whoa, that was nice!; and
- 3 - DAANNGG, I gotta learn those bars!

Juicy J & DJ Paul vs. Andre 3000

Ouch. I'm just going to put it out there – Andre 3000 is one of my Top 5 MCs (the others are Big Daddy Kane, Rakim, Black Thought, and Phonte). On the other hand, Three Six Mafia gets love from me due to their hustle and reinvention. Juicy J and DJ Paul are a case study in entrepreneurship. However, that's a study for another day; right now, Juicy J gets going with:

> *They call me the Juice and you know I'mma stunt*
> *Riding in the car with some bump in the trunk*
> *Tone in my lap & you know it's a pump*
> *Breaking down the good green, rolling the blunt*
> *Ghetto pimp type, girls say I'm the man*
> *Ice on the wrist with the ice in the chain*
> *Riding through the hood, got me gripping the grain*
> *And I'm sipping the same, while I'm changing the lane ...*

Consistent with the theme of the song, Juicy is fly. His flow is remarkable. He is in possession of that good stuff and in his fly-mobile, he is looking pretty cool. No surprises there. DJ Paul follows with:

> *DJ Paul is a dog, one you do not trust*
> *You leave your green around me, n***a your green gonna get lit up*
> *You leave your drank around me, believe your drank gonna get drunk up*
> *You leave your girl around me, if she bad she gonna get stuck ...*

Message: Do not leave your things unattended around DJ Paul.

Not even adding those verses together can touch a legendary verse from Andre 3000 as he flips the damn thang all the way over. I mean, getting married during an anthem for players? While wearing a kilt? Then on a track with a soulfully classic beat, he spits damn-near a cappella? Not only does he pull it off, man, he KILS the verse!

> *So, I typed a text to a girl I used to see*
> *Saying that I chose this cutie pie with whom I*
> *   wanna be*
> *And I apologize if this message gets you down*
> *Then I CC'ed every girl that I'd see-see*
> *   'round town*
> *And hate to see y'all frown but I'd rather see her*
> *   smilin'*
> *Wetness all around me, true, but I'm no island*
> *Peninsula maybe, it makes no sense, I know*
> *   crazy...*

The pairing of OutKast and UGK on the same track is heaven-sent and this verse from 3 Stacks steals the show.

> Juicy J & DJ Paul- 1 / Andre 3000 – 3
> "Stay Fly" – 1 / "International Player's Anthem" – 3

Young Buck & Crunchy Black vs. Pimp C

At the time "Stay Fly" dropped, Young Buck was on the come up – representing Nashville and G-Unit. Nowadays, that G-Unit affiliation has a little backlash for him but back when this song was bumping he was informing us of his bond with Three Six:

> *Three 6 Mafia, them my kinfolks*
> *So when I'm in Memphis, Tenn-a-key*
> *I just might not bring my own cause them n****s there*
> *Let me smoke for free.*

Crunchy Black follows Buck but doesn't add anything magical to the song.

True story: years before I penned old school Hip Hop flashbacks, I was a church administrator (not a preacher). Once, we were holding our weekly team meeting and the others noticed my downcast disposition. They inquired what was wrong and I responded, "Pimp C died." Yep, the rest of the team was speechless and you can see why I was not a preacher. Anyhow, ever since he crooned us about the stones filling up his pockets, Pimp C has held a special place in our Hip Hop memories. Here, he lives up to his name:

> *She be cross country, givin' all that she got*
> *A thousand a pop, I'm pullin' Bentleys off the lot*
> *I smashed up the gray one, bought me a red*
> *Every time we hit the parkin' lot we turn heads*
> *Some h**s wanna choose but them b*****s too scary*
> *Your b***h chose me, you ain't a pimp, you a fairy!*

You know the rules of the pimp game right? Well, if not, let's just say your lady choosing Pimp C (particularly during a song sampling "I Choose You") is not a good look for you.

Lyrically, Pimp breaks no new ground here even with his s***-talking bravado.

> Young Buck & Crunchy Black – 1 / Pimp C – 2
> "Stay Fly" – 2 / "International Player's Anthem" – 5

8Ball vs. Bun B

8Ball's and Bun B's impact on Southern Hip Hop cannot be overstated. While it is hard to push legacy aside, for this battle, we must. Even still, 8Ball's adheres his pimp legacy:

> *Your girlfriend wanna ride with me*
> *In a car with a pimp, where she supposed to be*
> *You ain't met no dude spit it cold as me ...*

If consistency matters, then 8Ball would win because he been laying down the pimp game since **Comin' Out Hard**. However, if we are going pimp bars vs. pimp bars then Bun B came out harder with:

> *Baby, you been rollin' solo, time to get down with*
>   *the team*
> *The grass is greener on that other side, if you*
>   *know what I mean*
> *I show you s*** you never seen, the Seven*
>   *Wonders of the World*
> *And I can make you the eighth if you wanna be*
>   *my girl...*

If we did a matchup of their respective catalogs, that head-to-head competition would be closer; but between these songs, we have to go with:

8Ball- 1 / Bun B – 2
"Stay Fly" – 3 / "International Player's Anthem" – 7

MJG vs. Big Boi

Much like his partner, 8Ball, MJG is known for spittin' pimp game. He is also known for his unique flow and underrated word play. Typically, in a relay, the anchor is leg is one of the teams strongest runners. MJG would prove that here as well, particularly considering his reputation as the closer as heard on the underground classic, "Lay It Down,"or the Bun-B track with 8Ball, David Banner, and Rick Ross, "You're Everything," and the slept-on club banger, "Sho'Nuff "with Tela. On "Stay Fly," MJG maintains his reputation as a closer with:

> *MJ finna sprinkle in some of that*
> *Super incredible, have a n***a running back*
> *Where that n***a with the hood sticky number at*
> *Cutting up a cigarillo like a lumber jack*
> *In the morning, when I need this and breath*
>   *again a whole lot of weed but*
> *I'm needing somebody to give me what I need*
> *When I want nothing less then the best of the*
>   *trees...*

Typing those words doesn't capture MJG's flow which takes the lyrics to a more memorable level. Speaking of flow, I'm an OutKast fan but I wasn't feeling Big Boi's flow on "International Player's Anthem." His emphasis on avoiding child support is advice to be heeded, but his wordplay is impeded by the flow:

> *Eeny meeny decisions, with precision I pick or*
> *Make my selection on who I choose to be wit', girl*
> *Don't touch my protection, I know you want it*
>   *to slip*
> *But slippin' is somethin' I don't do, tippin' for life.*

MJG – 2 / Big Boi – 1
"Stay Fly" – 5 / "International Player's Anthem" – 8

Having all those Tennessee legends on one track was genius and the beat? It's BANGIN'!!! Like for real, play it in your headphones during your workout and see if you don't get hype! Yet, UGK and OutKast on the same track? That's extraordinary. Though this beat also bumps, particularly as they change it up for each MC, it complements the MC more so than drives the song. With that in mind, lyrically? "International Player's Anthem" is the champ!

AFTERWORD

Revisiting these songs, the albums, the artists, and the memories has been like thumbing through an old photo album. Lots of laughs, tons of reflection, and effusive doses of nostalgia made it a joyous excursion. Yet, like all adventures, it comes to a close.

A few years back, Nicolay - one half of The Foreign Exchange, shared an online article that referenced the mid-30s as a time when we stop experimenting with new music and become entrenched in the music with which we are already familiar. To that point, the last "new" Hip Hop artist that I got attached to was Big K.R.I.T. Occasionally, I buy new Hip Hop - Apollo Brown and Rapsody come to mind; yet, the *I-will-be-at-the-record-store-as-soon-as-it-opens* feeling I had with Goodie Mob's **Soul Food** has long dissipated.

This phenomenon of aging through Hip Hop is represented through my own, my nephews, and my daughter's views of Lil' Wayne. To me, Lil' Wayne was the baby-faced kid in Juvenile's "Ha" video. I think I heard one song from his **Block Is Hot** album and incorrectly assumed he was a kid rapper like Lil' Bow Wow. My nephews are in their late

Afterword

20s and early 30s, to them, Lil' Wayne is the artist who blessed them with a steady stream of banging mixtapes. My teenaged daughters see Lil' Wayne as that old guy that either directly or indirectly (via Drake) influenced many of the Hip Hop artists they know. Artist of whom I often evoke Ice Cube's "they'll have a new ni*** next year" line to describe their staying power. However, the fact that Lil' Wayne has endured for this long is a testimony to the endurance and growth of the culture.

Not only does the music capture a time in our lives, the medium through which we experienced it also tells a part of our story. I'm old enough to remember my parents' eight tracks and the huge coffin-like console that was the record player in our living room. I remember walking to the record store to buy records. I remember shifting over to cassettes primarily to play them in the car or make primitive mixtapes from my records. I remember driving home from graduate school with my boom box CD player riding shotgun as I played the handful of CDs I owned then. I remember wondering if I would ever convert all my CDs, Records, & Tapes into a digital format.

Let's go back to those primitive mixtapes. One of which was a recording of WGPR's live radio broadcast from The Dancery nightclub in Detroit. I taped the segment to have some music from home as I headed away for college. During this particular broadcast, a promoter from Luke Records was present and being interviewed by Marvelous Marv, the host. As the promoter talked about the upcoming releases, Marv inquired as to whether he would be giving out any promotional items. The Luke Records guy shouted, "you know it! Records and Tapes!!"

That proclamation become an ongoing inside joke between me and Rashad when discussing buying new

Afterword

music. Now here we are, with a book that incorporates 'records and tapes' in the title and is a tangible manifestation of some outstanding Hip Hop memories.

Which brings me to the point that music evokes memories. I conclude this nostalgic book with the greatest Hip Hop song ever made playing in the background, "They Reminisce Over You (T.R.O.Y.)" by Pete Rock and CL Smooth. Yep, that's it exactly - these artists, these songs, and these memories are all worth reminiscing over.

> *It's like that y'all*
> *And you don't stop*
> *Pete rock and CL Smooth for '92*
> *And we out, later.*

ALSO BY SABIN PRENTIS

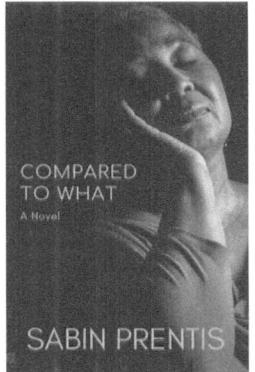

Compared To What

Better Left Unsaid

Assuming Hurts

Fred Duncan with Sabin Duncan

Four Floors

ABOUT THE AUTHOR

Sabin Prentis is a husband, father, educator, native Detroiter, and Creator of Literary Soul Food. He is the owner of Fielding Books and the author of *Assuming Hurts*, *Better Left Unsaid*, *Compared To What*, *Reflections from the Frontline*, and co-author of *Listen Up* and *Four Floors*.

For more information, visit:
sabinprentis.com

www.ingramcontent.com/pod-product-compliance
Lightning Source LLC
Chambersburg PA
CBHW030435010526
44118CB00011B/647